Women and Entrepreneurship

To my children, Renato and Raffaella, my life's great treasures.
They are my source of inspiration for everything I undertake in life.
To my husband, my love partner in life.
For my mother and father, to whom I owe everything I am in life.
Beatrice E. Avolio Alecchi

To the memory of my beloved parents,
who showed me how to find strength and wisdom in my life.
This book is also dedicated to my husband Dusan and son Milos,
who are always my inspiration. I love you all!
Mirjana Radović-Marković

Women and Entrepreneurship

Female Durability, Persistence and Intuition at Work

BEATRICE E. AVOLIO ALECCHI
CENTRUM Católica, Peru

MIRJANA RADOVIĆ-MARKOVIĆ
Akamai University, USA

GOWER

Gower Applied Business Research
Our programme provides leaders, practitioners, scholars and researchers with thought provoking, cutting edge books that combine conceptual insights, interdisciplinary rigour and practical relevance in key areas of business and management.

Published by
Gower Publishing Limited
Wey Court East
Union Road
Farnham
Surrey, GU9 7PT
England

Ashgate Publishing Company
110 Cherry Street
Suite 3-1
Burlington, VT 05401-3818
USA

www.gowerpublishing.com

British Library Cataloguing in Publication Data
A catalogue record for this book is available from the British Library.

The Library of Congress has cataloged the printed edition as follows:
Alecchi, Beatrice E. Avolio.
  Women and entrepreneurship : female durability, persistence and intuition
at work / by Beatrice E Avolio Alecchi and Mirjana Radovic-Markovic.
      pages cm
  Includes bibliographical references and index.
  ISBN 978-1-4094-6618-5 (hardback) -- ISBN 978-1-4094-6619-2 (ebook) -- ISBN 978-1-4094-6620-8 (epub) 1. Self-employed women. 2. Businesswomen. 3. Women-owned business enterprises. 4. Entrepreneurship. I. Markovic, Mirjana Radovic. II. Title.

  HD6072.5.A45 2013
  338'.04082--dc23

2013008806

ISBN 9781409466185 (hbk)
ISBN 9781409466192 (ebk – PDF)
ISBN 9781409466208 (ebk – ePUB)

Printed in the United Kingdom by Henry Ling Limited, at the Dorset Press, Dorchester, DT1 1HD

Contents

List of Figures and Tables

Figures

Tables

About the Authors

Dr Beatrice E. Avolio Alecchi

Dr Beatrice Avolio Alecchi holds a PhD in Strategic Business Administration from the Pontificia Universidad Católica del Peru and a Doctorate in Business Administration from Maastricht School of Management, the Netherlands. She has also obtained a M.Phil. from Maastricht School of Management, the Netherlands and an MBA from The Graduate School of Business Administration, ESAN, in Lima, Peru. She obtained a Bachelor degree in Business Administration and a Bachelor degree in Accounting from the Universidad del Pacífico in Lima, Peru.

Dr Avolio is co-author of the books *Rutas Hacia un Perú Mejor, Qué Hacer y Cómo Lograrlo* [*Routes to a Better Peru: What to Do and How to Achieve It*] (Editorial Aguilar, 2010); *Planeamiento Estratégico para la Gastronomía Peruana* [*Strategic Planning for Peruvian Gastronomy*] (Gerencial al Día, Pearson Educación, 2008); *Cajamarca Competitiva* [*Competitive Cajamarca*] (Saywa Ediciones, 1998); *Perú: Destino de Inversiones 1997–1998* [*Peru: A Place to Invest 1997–1998*] (ESAN Ediciones, 1997); *Crisis* (CENTRUM Católica, 2010); and *Financial Accounting* (Cengage Education, 2011).

Dr Avolio's doctoral dissertation was entitled "A Profile of Women Entrepeneurs in Peru: An Exploratory Study". She is also the author of many academic articles, among others: "Las limitaciones de la información contable" [The limitations of accounting information] (Gestión, 2000), "Métodos de valorización de empresas" [Methods of company valuation] and "Hacia una sociedad de mujeres empresarias" [Towards a society of female entrepreneurs]; and has written articles in newspapers and specialized magazines, including, "Los Retos de las mujeres emprendedoras" [The challenges of female entrepreneurs] (Strategia, 2009); "Las Mujeres Empresarias en el Perú" [Businesswomen in Peru] (Editorial Norma, forthcoming); and "Por qué las Mujeres se Convierten en Empresarias" [Why women become entrepreneurs] (forthcoming).

She is the founder of the Center for Female Entrepreneurs at CENTRUM Católica and is conducting research on female entrepreneurs and executives in Latin America, including the role of female executives in large companies, the role of the entrepreneur's partner and factors that hinder company growth.

Dr Avolio has been a Financial Analyst at Southern Peru Ltd., an international mining company; an Advisor at Price Waterhouse; and Chair of the departments of Finance, Accounting and Economics at business schools. Her areas of specialization include Finance and Business Management, Financial Planning and Entrepreneurship. Dr Avolio is currently Deputy Director General of CENTRUM Católica and Professor of Finance and Entrepreneurship at CENTRUM Católica.

Dr Mirjana Radović-Marković

Academician Dr Mirjana Radović-Marković is a full professor of Entrepreneurship at Akamai University (Director of Master studies and a member of the Board of Directors, Akamai University, United States); Faculty of Business Economics and Entrepreneurship, Serbia; and Institute of Economic Sciences. She holds a BSc; MSc and PhD degrees in Economics, as well as post-doctoral studies in multidisciplinary studies. After completing her dissertation, she continued her advanced studies in the Netherlands, United States and Russia. She visited famous universities in the United States (Stanford University, Columbia University, University of Pittsburgh), and gave lectures at Lomonosow (Russia) and recently, at Oxford University (UK), Franklin College (Lugano, Switzerland), OECD Experts' meeting on the Black Sea and Central Asia Initiative held in Instanbul (Turkey), and at the Faculty of Economics, University in Miškolc, Hungary.

She holds the Honorary Doctorate of Science (DSc) from St James the Elder Theological Seminary, Tennessee, United States (2010) and the Honorary Doctorate of Letters (DLitt.) from the Academy of Universal Global Peace, Chennai, India (2010). The awarding committees cited Dr Radović-Marković for having served the world community with outstanding research in Economics and Women's Entrepreneurship.

Dr Mirjana Radović-Marković is a Fellow (academician) of the Academia Europea, London (UK), World Academy of Art and Science (United States), the Euro Mediterranean Academy of Arts and Sciences, Athens (Greece), and the Royal Society of the Arts (RSA) in London (UK).

Foreword

I have the honour and privilege to write the Foreword for this book because I have worked closely with one of the authors (*Dr Mirjana Radović-Marković*) in three publications and various peer-reviewed articles on women entrepreneurship.

In this book, we can see the application of the authors' long academic and professional experience as lecturers and researchers. The authors have an especially rich experience in this field of research, the results of which are included in this book. Here, they present the latest results from their research on women entrepreneurs and their positions in the business world.

The increased participation of women in business leadership has brought about completely new ways of business communication, and effective new business strategies and company development models have been proven. In particular, as a consequence of women entering fields of business that were traditionally dominated by men, women have used their advantages, durability and persistence in the work place, and, above all, intuition in making business decisions, thus contributing new business advantages. At the same time, they have changed traditional opinions of the roles of women in business, thus imposing the new behavioural style into business.

This book also discusses the core issues involved in deciding to pursue an entrepreneurial vision, and what characteristics are vital to success from the very beginning. It will serve as a catalyst to motivate business ideas from the very beginning to their being put into practice. In addition, it will help modern women as entrepreneurs to form opinions about the overall business climate and how their ideas might fare under current economic conditions.

As they become more convinced of the potential of their business ideas, they are led to delve deeper into specifics that will ultimately become part of a formal business plan. In addition, the authors discuss different types of businesses and ways they are conducted. They stress the fact that "businesses that entrepreneurs do at their homes are relatively new" (Radović-Marković, Chapter 11). These are usually smaller businesses that provide intellectual and other services. According to many indexes, those businesses are very stable, which is affirmed by data showing that the average age of a business that owners run from their home is around six years. In addition to helping people generate ideas for home businesses, the authors provide advice on a wide range of topics affecting home-based business owners.

The book is written in simple and plain language and this will help the process of understanding for beginning students of entrepreneurial studies and likewise for other users.

Prof. Dr M.A. Omolaja,
President, ICMT International and IPFM, Great Britain

Preface

We decided to write this book in order to deepen current knowledge on female entrepreneurship. During our academic and professional experience to date we have had the opportunity to work closely with women who are starting businesses and also with women who have been successfully operating their enterprises for many years. We have realized that the experience, typology, motives and characteristics of female entrepreneurs are different from those of male entrepreneurs.

Despite the fact that women have gained an important role in economic, political and social domains there is still a marked gap between men and women, not only in the field of entrepreneurship but also more generally in terms of economic, political and social development. Given the particular experiences for women when starting and operating a business, it is necessary to thoroughly understand female entrepreneurship in order to be able to help women to become independent and successful entrepreneurs.

This book presents a major study of female entrepreneurs in a developing country in Latin America, which explores thoroughly the experience of women and their enterprises. Through the analysis of this case study and its comparison with other studies from other countries a conceptual framework is proposed to explain the various factors that have stimulated women to choose entrepreneurial activity.

We then present a series of chapters on emerging topics in entrepreneurship which aid a comprehensive understanding of female entrepreneurs. Here we focus on the sorts of entrepreneurship and kinds of businesses that are key to alleviating poverty by giving women, in particular, tools and opportunities enabling them to have independent economic income and a source of empowerment and fulfillment.

Acknowledgements

We are grateful to the book reviewers: Professor Dr Dragoš Simandan, Brock University, Canada; and Professor Dr Muhammad Omolaja, ICMT and IPFM, Great Britain.

We are also thankful to our families and academic institutions to which we belong, CENTRUM Católica (Peru) and Akamai University (United States). This book would not have been possible without their support.

PART I

Female Entrepreneurship

Introduction

In the first part of the book we explore the characteristics, motives and profiles of women entrepreneurs. To begin with, we analyse the theoretical background of entrepreneurship examining a series of studies focused on the definition of entrepreneurship and current literature on women entrepreneurs and their enterprises. This is complemented with a case study to obtain information and knowledge on women entrepreneurs; identifying the factors that motivate women. As a result we have developed a conceptual framework to explain various factors that have stimulated women to choose entrepreneurial activities, which amount to a complex system of circumstances and motives.

The case study focuses on women entrepreneurs from a Latin American country. We decided to focus on an emerging country in Latin America as its political and economic context is similar to other emerging countries. Furthermore, women entrepreneurs face similar challenges regardless of the country they live in.

To complete this first part we explore and discuss different issues derived from female entrepreneurship. We analyse the new role of women as entrepreneurs and the obstacles they face as they have to balance work and family and deal with gender inequalities. We also examine the special topic of women in the labour market.

Female Entrepreneurship: Theoretical Background

Introduction

Entrepreneurship is an emerging research area among academics because it is acknowledged that fostering entrepreneurial activity is associated with greater economic growth (Weeks and Seiler, 2001). Specifically, the interest in understanding women's entrepreneurial activity is a result of the importance they are gaining in the entrepreneurial sector as well as evidence that women encounter difficulties in starting and operating a business that are different from those faced by men (Neider, 1987).

The initial research on women entrepreneurs was focused on understanding their background and the organizational characteristics of their enterprises. The most recent studies take into consideration more extensive research studies on the problems they face, their administrative practices, the perceptions of women as entrepreneurs, their skills for success, gender differences, conflicts between their roles in their enterprises and their families, and the vision they have for their enterprises. Methodologically, most research studies were based on surveys and case studies. They are mainly descriptive and use convenience samples as there are no databases of women entrepreneurs. In addition, research is frequently not associated with any base theory. However, such studies have made it possible to obtain knowledge, with which theories on women's entrepreneurial activity are developing.

This chapter presents the current literature on women entrepreneurs and their enterprises. The subject has been organized into general and specific aspects. Initially, the literature on entrepreneurship in general, the growth of women's entrepreneurial activity and the main results of the international research studies are presented.

The term *entrepreneurship* is defined as: "The state of being an entrepreneur or the activities associated with being an entrepreneur" (HarperCollins, 2003). There is not an agreement on the translation of the term entrepreneurship to Spanish. Some studies use *espíritu empresarial* (HarperCollins, 2005), *empresarialidad* (Argentina) or *emprendedorismo* (Brazil and papers elaborated by the Inter-American Development Bank) (United States Agency of International Development (USAID), 2005).

The study of entrepreneurship has become one of the fastest growing fields of research in recent decades as a result of the recognition that it will increase local capabilities to bring economic growth and help to develop the market economy (Weeks and Seiler, 2001). There is evidence that promoting entrepreneurial activity, and in particular women's entrepreneurial activity, is related to economic growth. According to the National Foundation of Women Business Owners (quoted by Weeks and Seiler, 2001, p. 5), there is a positive and important correlation between participation by women who are employers or self-employed and the growth of the Gross Domestic Product (GDP). According to Weeks and Seiler (2001), data from previous research may be imperfect, but:

> *Analysis of the relationship between women's economic activity in general, their managerial status and entrepreneurial activity and national economic growth throughout Latin America and the Caribbean shows that support for entrepreneurial development efforts could have a significant impact on economic growth and prosperity in the region. (p. i)*

According to *Global Entrepreneurship Monitor: 2004 Report on Women and Entrepreneurship* by Minniti et al. (2005), entrepreneurial activity plays a very important role in the creation of an active and dynamic economy, especially entrepreneurial activity by women, whose role is analysed in this study both in developed and developing economies. For both men and women, opportunity is the main motive to start enterprises; however, many women start their own enterprises as a result of a lack of opportunities in the workplace. In low-income countries, women who get involved in entrepreneurial activities are usually between 25 and 34 years old, while in high-income countries, they tend to be between 35 and 44 years old. The findings of the study concluded that the creation of governmental policies to support education, financial aid, networking and enterprise counselling permits women to be increasingly involved in the development of new enterprises.

What is an Entrepreneur?

The term *entrepreneur* is difficult to define as there is no accepted definition in either academic or in common language.

Entrepreneurship has been studied by several disciplines, including sociology, psychology and economics; resulting in different definitions in each. Some studies consider entrepreneurs to be: (a) only people who establish new enterprises (Bennett and Dann, 2000; Hisrich and Brush, 1986; Inman, 2000; Schwartz, 1976; Smith-Hunter, 2003), while others refer to enterprise owners without taking into account how they obtained ownership of them (Aidis, 2002; Izyumov and Razumnova, 2000); (b) only people who are employers (Hisrich and Fulop, 1994; Inman, 2000; Smith-Hunter, 2003) or self-employed (Aidis, 2002; Izyumov and Razumnova, 2000; Voeten, 2002a); (c) people who not only own, but also manage their enterprises (Aidis, 2002; Inman, 2000; Lee-Gosselin and Grisé, 1990), or who own but do not manage their business (Bennett and Dann, 2000); (d) only people who establish a business in order to obtain profits and growth (Bennett and Dann, 2000), excluding small business proprietors, who are defined as "… those who establish and administrate a business with the main objective of achieving personal goals; where the business is the main source of income and consumes most of their time and resources, and where the proprietor sees the business as an extension of their own personality and is related to their family needs" (Carland et al., 1984, p. 358).

Given the importance of the definition of entrepreneur, we will compile a variety of definitions used in previous studies in order to conceptualize different related aspects

DEFINITIONS OF ENTREPRENEUR

The term *entrepreneur* comes from the French verb *entreprendre*, which means *"undertake"*. The concept appeared for the first time in 1437 in the *French Dictionnaire de la Langue Française* and it was associated with the adventurers who travelled in search of opportunities or with men who undertook military expeditions (Landstrom, 1999).

At the basic level, an entrepreneur is defined as "someone who starts their own business, especially when this involves risks" (Cambridge University Press, 2008) and "a person who owns and runs a business – not necessarily a new, small, growing or successful business" (Oxford University Press, 1998).

These definitions emphasize the entrepreneur as the proprietor of a business without making any distinction on the way such proprietorship was acquired, and not excluding self-employment from the concept of entrepreneur.

From an economic perspective, the entrepreneur is related with risk and defined as "a person who risks capital and other resources in the hope of substantial financial gain" (Oxford University Press, 1998). From a sociological perspective an entrepreneur is defined as an innovative individual: "… entrepreneurship, as defined, essentially, consists in doing things that are not generally done in ordinary course of business routine" (Schumpeter, 1934, p. 254).

DEFINITIONS USED IN RESEARCH

Schwartz (1976) defined an entrepreneur as "an innovative individual who creates and builds a business from nonexistence" (p. 47), which implies that an entrepreneur creates a new enterprise. Hisrich and Brush (1986) define an entrepreneur as a person who "creates something different and valuable, devoting the necessary time and effort, assuming financial, psychological and social risks, and receiving monetary remuneration and personal satisfaction" (p. 4). Aidis (2002) believes that the concept of entrepreneur is connected with innovative behaviour, a situation that may not be present in enterprises at a moment in time and that is difficult to prove. The term *business proprietor* was preferred in Aidis's study, that is, individuals who have their own businesses and are actively involved in its operation. This definition does not take into account how proprietorship was obtained or distinguish between employer and self-employed (self-employment considers the owner as the only worker).

Lee-Gosselin and Grisé (1990) studied women entrepreneurs in Canada and operationalized the term *women entrepreneur* according to the following criteria: women who own at least 1 per cent of the enterprise's property, are responsible for at least one managerial function (marketing, accounting, human resources or other) and work in the enterprise. Inman (2000) studied Afro-American women entrepreneurs in the United States and applied the following criteria: women should own more than 51 per cent of the business, have less than 500 employees, have founded the business (he excluded bought or inherited enterprises), administer their business, work full time in the enterprise and receive the majority of their income from the enterprise.

Bennett and Dann (2000) defined an entrepreneur as "a person who has established the enterprise as a new venture, where growth is intended, for the prime reasons of generating profit and achieving personal satisfaction" (p. 78). To operationalize this definition, the authors divided the term into three parts: create a new enterprise, guide it towards growth and motivation. According to Izyumov and Razumnova (2000), any business in Russia is an entrepreneurial adventure as a result of the lack of financial and legal infrastructure, and the associated personal risk. Therefore, these authors use without distinction the terms *microenterprise, small business, self-employment and entrepreneur*, given that in transitional economies such as Russia's, the distinction between these terms is unclear.

An interesting approach is used in Vietnam as part of Phase 2 of the Training for Women in Micro and Small Enterprises project (Voeten, 2002a) in order to distinguish women entrepreneurs from those involved in commercial activities in order to survive. The document developed a set of criteria to classify women: if it is or not a women's enterprise; if women were pushed or pulled into the enterprise; if women would leave the enterprise if they were offered a permanent job; whether the enterprise is formally established; whether they are willing to pay for training in administrative matters; whether they wish to expand their enterprises; whether they hire personnel; whether they take risks or reinvest in their enterprises; whether the enterprise's and personal finances are separated; whether the business has some kind of accounting record. The study argues that, to be considered a entrepreneur, a woman should be *pushed* into the creation of the company, she should not leave her company if offered a permanent job elsewhere, her business should be formalized, she should be willing to pay for training in administrative activities, she should seek expansion of her businesses and hire labour, take risks and reinvest in her business, and the finances of the business must be separate from personal finances.

Smith-Hunter (2003) made the analysis according to the dimensions of the proprietor of a small business, and separated the concepts of *entrepreneur, manager, self-employed* and *employee*.

For Steinhoff and Burguess (1989, quoted in Smith-Hunter, 2003), an *entrepreneur* is a "person who organizes, runs and takes the risks involved in operating a business" (p. 14). For Stoner and Freeman (1992, quoted in Smith-Hunter, 2003) a *manager* is "someone who has formal authority to play a series of impersonal, informational and decision-making roles in a particular unit" (p. 13). An entrepreneur is associated with the creation of a new business, according to Smith-Hunter (2003), and they may or may not choose to manage it. If they chose not to manage it, the entrepreneur would only be an investor.

The self-employed are persons who work for themselves ("not working for an employer but finding work for oneself") (Cambridge University Press, 2003). Under this concept, even when the *proprietor of the business* is regarded as self-employed, a self-employed individual is not necessarily the owner of a business. To be considered as the proprietor of a business, the business must be established as an enterprise, that is, an organization that pursues certain ends. Individuals who work for themselves and who have not constituted an enterprise are self-employed, but they are not proprietors of a business (Smith-Hunter, 2003).

The *employee* dimension is closely linked to the enterprise dimension. An employee is someone who for a salary or wage carries out domestic work or helps in a business (Real Academia Española, 2001). While the owners of some enterprises take their income from the profit of the business, others choose to assign themselves a salary for their job, also turning themselves into employees.

Taking these dimensions into account, Smith-Hunter (2003) considers that the proprietors of an enterprise run their business as administrators; they risk, invest and create businesses as entrepreneurs; they employ themselves, and they are also employees in their own business should they assign a salary for themselves. "This multi-dimensional view of the small business owner is extremely important because it allows a look at the complex nature of the various dimensions of the small business proprietor" (Smith-Hunter, 2003, p. 16).

Why Study Women Entrepreneurs?

Since the 1970s and 1980s, there has been a growing interest in studying women entrepreneurs, mainly in the United States and Canada, as a result of the high growth in the number of enterprises created by women and also because it was thought that women encounter difficulties in starting and operating businesses that are different from those faced by men (Neider, 1987).

Carter and Cannon (1992) criticized those who said that the results of studies on men entrepreneurs could be applied to the case of women entrepreneurs. Hisrich and Brush (1984) considered that most of the knowledge on entrepreneurial activity is based on studies about men entrepreneurs. Brush and Bird (2002) showed that theories on the creation of organizations have been generated and tested on men entrepreneurs. For them, these approaches do not necessarily reflect women's processes and organizational styles because "women and men manage their enterprises in different ways, they use different strategies and organizational structures" (p. 42).

Hisrich and Brush (1986) demonstrated that women-owned enterprises are more dissimilar than similar to those owned by men. They showed that women and men entrepreneurs have similar personalities and background, except for the fact that most women are older when they get involved in an entrepreneurial venture: 35 to 45 years old instead of 25 to 35 years old in the case of men. There are differences, however, in their motivations, the processes involved when starting their enterprises, their administrative and entrepreneurial skills, professional background and the problems they face:

> *Men entrepreneurs are usually motivated by the desire to control their own destiny, whereas women tend to be motivated by a need of independence and achievement as a result of the frustration they feel by not being able to perform at work at the level they know they could. Occupationally, men tend to be more competitive in their business management skills, and women usually have limited administrative experience at medium level and in service areas. (p. 15)*

Zapalska (1997) studied women entrepreneurs in Poland and found that they are significantly different to men in important dimensions; therefore they require assistance plans specially developed for their specific needs. He found that there are significant differences in the obstacles they face, the reasons they have to start a business, their goals and the factors they consider important for their success.

Minniti et al. (2005) showed that men's and women's entrepreneurial attitudes are influenced by several of the same variables, but all these factors do not influence both genders in the same way or with the same intensity. In this way, the decision of starting an enterprise has a different level of complexity for women and for men. In addition, women tend to be more sensitive than men regarding non-monetary incentives:

> *For women more than men, the decision of starting a new enterprise is usually related with need or the flexibility of the hours or location; that is to say, the kind of independence that allows them to conciliate family needs and child care. (p. 15)*

Mitchell (2004) studied the motivation of women entrepreneurs in South Africa, and showed that starting an enterprise involves a significant amount of risk and effort for any entrepreneur. For women, however, the risk is higher because they not only have the usual problems related to the enterprises, but they also have to solve the problems of being a woman in a society dominated by men. Modern research studies indicate that women face different problems to men entrepreneurs and that "it is imperative that a better understanding of women entrepreneurs and the specific constrains they face in starting or operating a business is made, so as to develop appropriate assistance programs and policies" (p. 170).

Moreover, experts say that any activity aiming to confront economic and socio-cultural crisis in a society must incorporate women, because the improvement of their life situation has direct multiplier effects on their families and children because of the three roles that are part of most women's life: the role of mother, which is the driving force of their actions; the role of wife, as a source of support, backing and, sometimes, source of conflict or frustrations; and the role of productive agent, who assumes economic responsibility for her family (Ministerio de Industria, Turismo, Integración y Negociaciones Comerciales Internacionales (MITINCI), 1997).

Women Entrepreneurial Activity

The Center for Women's Business Research (n.d. 2006) of the United States provides the most comprehensive information available on women entrepreneurs in that country, and offers estimates of the impact of their enterprises on the economy of the United States. According to this data, two out of every five enterprises (40.2 per cent) in the United States are 50 per cent or more owned by women, with a total of 10.4 million enterprises (estimate as of 2006). Women's enterprises contribute 1.9 million dollars in annual sales and hire 12.8 million people. Close to 19 per cent of women's enterprises have employees, and the ratio is similar to all enterprises in the United States (19 per cent versus 25 per cent). The estimate of the total cost of salaries and wages in women's enterprises was 546 billion dollars in 2006. Between 1997 and 2006, women's enterprises grew twice as fast as other enterprises (42.3 per cent versus 23.3 per cent) in the United States. In 2006, the highest proportion of women-owned enterprises (in which women have a participation of over 51 per cent in the enterprise) was in the service sector, with 69 per cent; followed by 14.4 per cent in the retail business, and 7.7 per cent in real estate, rents and leasing.

Minniti et al. (2005), prepared at the Center for Women's Leadership of Babson College in the United States, has the most complete information available on women's entrepreneurial activity in the world. According to the study, the number of women-owned enterprises is increasing all over the world. Women-owned enterprises represent between a quarter and a third of the enterprises in the formal economy, and it seems they have an even more important role in the informal sectors.

The study presents statistics of the female Total Entrepreneurial Activity (TEA) rate, and defines entrepreneurship as "Any attempt of creating a new business or the creation of new enterprises, such as self-employment, reorganization of a business or the expansion of already existent business by an individual or group of individuals or already established enterprise" (Serida et al., 2005, p. 13). TEA measures the percentage of adults between 18 and 64 years that own all or part of a business for less than 42 months, and includes *incipient enterprises* as well as *new enterprises*. An enterprise is considered incipient if the proprietors of all or part of a business have paid wages or salaries for not more than three months or have taken specific actions to start the business. An enterprise is considered new if the proprietors of all or part of a business they actively manage have paid remunerations for more than three months, but less than 42 (Serida et al., 2005).

In the study carried out by Minniti et al. (2005), female TEA varies significantly among the 34 countries studied; from Peru's 39.1 per cent to Japan's 1.2 per cent. This study analysed the motivations that women have to become entrepreneurs. *Entrepreneurship by opportunity* refers to when people have decided to start their own business or enterprise as a desirable career option, and this reflects the desire to take advantage of an entrepreneurial opportunity. *Entrepreneurship by need* refers to people who start their own business because other employment options are either absent or unsatisfactory. Results indicated that, as for men, most women start their own business or enterprises in order take advantage of an opportunity. Women who choose the entrepreneurial activity because of need are concentrated in low-income countries. This study also provides information to establish a profile of women entrepreneurs in the world regarding: (a) demographic and socio-economic factors like age, education, working situation and presence of models; and (b) subjective factors like fear of failure, perception of opportunity and confidence in their skills.

According to Weeks (2001, quoted by Baycan et al., 2003, p. 6), between a quarter and a third of formal enterprises are the property of women and are run by them. In the United States (in 1999), they represented 38 per cent; in Finland (in 1990), 34 per cent; in Australia (in 1994) and Canada (in 1996), 33 per cent; in Korea (in 1998), 32 per cent; and in Mexico (in 1997), 30 per cent of enterprises.

Women Entrepreneurs in the World

The research on women entrepreneurs is quite broad in developed countries, especially in the United States, Canada and the United Kingdom, because there is not much knowledge of women and their enterprises in Latin America and, especially, in Peru. There are specific studies in France, Singapore, Russia, Ireland, Puerto Rico, China, Turkey, Hungary, South Africa, Israel, Poland, Germany, India, Lithuania, Greece and Australia.

Tables 1.1, 1.2 and 1.3 list the principal studies that have been carried out on women entrepreneurs. In order to analyse the main trends of these studies, the articles have been classified according to the conceptual framework of Gartner (1985) for the creation of new enterprises: individual, environment, organization and processes.

Most studies on women entrepreneurs have focused on the individual. The initial studies were devoted to knowing the background and organizational characteristics of their enterprises; most recent studies consider wider research on the problems faced by women entrepreneurs, their administrative practices, perceptions of women as administrators, their abilities for achieving success, gender differences, conflicts between their roles in their enterprises and their families, and the vision they have for their enterprises. Methodologically, most studies are based on surveys and case studies, they are mainly descriptive and use convenience samples as there are no databases on women entrepreneurs, and they frequently do not associate research with theory. Other methodological issues include a lack of instrument validation, the existence of a sole source of information, a tendency to generalize on the behaviour and characteristics of different types of women (women that create new enterprises, women that take charge of the family business, differences in ages, industries, size) (Brush, 1992). Despite all these, such studies have produced knowledge on the basis of which theories are being developed on women's entrepreneurial activity.

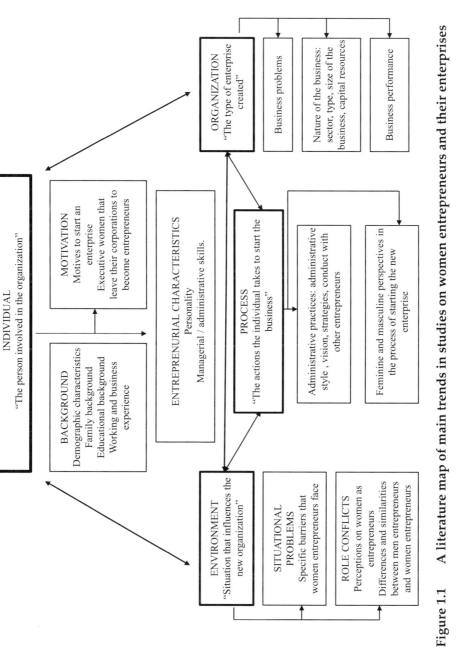

Figure 1.1   A literature map of main trends in studies on women entrepreneurs and their enterprises

INDIVIDUAL
"The person involved in the organization"

BACKGROUND
Demographic characteristics
Family background
Educational background
Working and business experience

MOTIVATION
Motives to start an enterprise
Executive women that leave their corporations to become entrepreneurs

ENTREPRENURIAL CHARACTERISTICS
Personality
Managerial / administrative skills.

ENVIRONMENT
"Situation that influences the new organization"

SITUATIONAL PROBLEMS
Specific barriers that women entrepreneurs face

ROLE CONFLICTS
Perceptions on women as entrepreneurs
Differences and similarities between men entrepreneurs and women entrepreneurs

PROCESS
"The actions the individual takes to start the business"

Administrative practices: administrative style, vision, strategies, conduct with other entrepreneurs

Feminine and masculine perspectives in the process of starting the new enterprise

ORGANIZATION
"The type of enterprise created"

Business problems

Nature of the business: sector, type, size of the business, capital resources

Business performance

Figure 1.1 shows the map of the literature and presents the main trends that have arisen from the research on women entrepreneurs and their enterprises. The individual aspects refer to the person involved in creating the new organization and include demographic aspects, background, motivations, working and educational experiences, and psychological aspects. The organization refers to the type of enterprise created, and includes strategy, organizational characteristics, type of enterprise, structure and problems faced. The process refers to the actions taken by the entrepreneur to start the enterprise, and includes the identification of opportunities, the search for resources, the construction of the organization, the administration of the enterprise and the response to the environment. Environment is the situation affecting and influencing the organization, and includes legal, politic, governmental, sector and technological aspects (Gartner, 1985).

Table 1.1   List of research related to individual and organizational aspects of women entrepreneurs

Topic	Country	Author	Year
Individual Aspects			
Background and differences by type of business	USA	Hisrich and O'Brien	1982
Typology of women entrepreneurs	UK	Goffee and Scase	1985
Background	USA	Bowen and Hisrich	1986
Background, motivations, administrative skills	USA	Hisrich and Brush	1986
Motivations for starting a business	Several countries	Scheinberg and MacMillan	1988
Reasons for failure or success of management by women entrepreneurs	Chile	Pardo and Gómez	1990
Typology of women entrepreneurs	UK	Carter and Cannon	1992
Motivations to start the business	Australia	Langan-Fox and Roth	1995
Motivations to start the business	Singapore	Lee	1996
Motivational influences in the decisions of entrepreneurs	USA	Moore and Buttner	1997
Women entrepreneurs as a source of economic growth	Argentina	NFWBO	2000
Motivations for starting a business	France	Orhan and Scott	2001
Family–work conflict	Singapore	Siew Kim and Seow Ling	2001
Effects of training on women entrepreneurs	Vietnam	Voeten, 2002a Voeten, 2002b	2002

Topic	Country	Author	Year
Family–work conflict	USA, South Africa	Schindehutte et al.	2003
Motivational influences in professional women and their entrepreneurial decisions	USA	Mattis	2004
Organizational Aspects			
Business problems	Poland	Mroczkowski	1997
Growth pattern of women businesses	India	Mitra	2002

Table 1.2   List of research related to both individual and organizational aspects of women entrepreneurs

Topic	Country	Author	Year
Motivations, management style, business problems	USA	Schwartz	1976
Background and business organizational characteristics	USA	Cooper and Dunkelberg	1981
Background, motivations and business problems	USA	Hisrich and O'Brien	1981
Background, business problems	USA	Hisrich and Brush	1984
Background and business organizational characteristics	USA, Puerto Rico, Ireland	Hisrich	1986
Background and business organizational characteristics	USA	Neider	1987
Background, business success factors	USA	Hisrich and Brush	1991
Background, nature of the business	China	Hisrich and Fan	1991
Background, business problems	Hungary	Hisrich and Fulop	1994
Documents of the Conference "Women Entrepreneurs" carried out at the University of Bradford in May 1989	UK	Allen and Truman	1993
Individual factors and business performance	Israel	Hisrich et al.	1997
Demographic characteristics, skills	Poland	Zapalska	1997
Background, motivations, business problems, administrative skills	Turkey	Hisrich and Ayse Öztürk	1999
Demographic characteristics, education, motivations, resources and planning	Australia	Bennett and Dann	2000
Background, motivations, obstacles, organizational characteristics	Arab Countries	Dechant and Al Lamky	2005

Table 1.3   List of research related to situational aspects and the processes by which the enterprise is created

Topic	Country	Author	Year
Motivations, management style, business problems	USA	Schwartz	1976
Background and business organizational characteristics	USA	Cooper and Dunkelberg	1981
Background, motivations and business problems	USA	Hisrich and O'Brien	1981
Background, business problems	USA	Hisrich and Brush	1984
Background and business organizational characteristics	USA, Puerto Rico, Ireland	Hisrich	1986
Background and business organizational characteristics	USA	Neider	1987
Background, business success factors	USA	Hisrich and Brush	1991
Background, nature of the business	China	Hisrich and Fan	1991
Background, business problems	Hungary	Hisrich and Fulop	1994
Documents of the Conference "Women Entrepreneurs" carried out at the University of Bradford in May 1989	UK	Allen and Truman	1993
Individual factors and business performance	Israel	Hisrich et al.	1997
Demographic characteristics, skills	Poland	Zapalska	1997
Background, motivations, business problems, administrative skills	Turkey	Hisrich and Ayse Öztürk	1999
Demographic characteristics, education, motivations, resources and planning	Australia	Bennett and Dann	2000
Background, motivations, obstacles, organizational characteristics	Arab Countries	Dechant and Al Lamky	2005

Hisrich and Brush (1984) identified the typical profile of women entrepreneurs with a national survey of 468 women in the United States. They found that women entrepreneurs have similar family background, education, work experience, entrepreneurial characteristics, administrative skills and motivation; and that most women entrepreneurs were firstborns in middle-class families where the father was self-employed. Almost half of them are married to men working in professional or technical activities and have, on average, two adolescent children. Almost 70 per cent of women entrepreneurs have basic education, and many have university degrees; their parents and husbands also have a high level of education. Most of them do not have administrative knowledge; thus 90 per cent start enterprises in the service sector. Besides, typical women entrepreneurs have limited working experience, and when they do, it is in service areas like teaching, intermediate-level administrative positions or as secretaries.

Their enterprises are small in terms of sales and employees. Hisrich and Fan (1991) quote a study made of 17,000 women entrepreneurs in Europe, of which more than half have no employees, 20 per cent employ family members and only 25 per cent employ workers outside the family. Women entrepreneurs are individualist, creative, enthusiastic, instinctive and adaptable. In general, they have the same characteristics as men entrepreneurs: they have a lot of energy, they are independent, they have confidence in themselves, and they are competitive and results-oriented (Hisrich and Fan, 1991).

Women Entrepreneurs in Latin America

The United Nations (1995, quoted by Weeks and Seiler, 2001), has gathered information on women's business activity, though the information is often imperfect, either being from different years or being different from information from other countries. According to this information, the three key indicators of the role played by women in Latin America are their Rate of Economic Activity, the percentage of women employees in the administrative/managerial area and their rate of self-employment.

The Rate of Economic Activity refers to those people over 15 years old who are working or looking for a job, and whose work is not necessarily paid (for example, in the case of agriculture, it may be for subsistence). Regarding self-employment, this indicator takes into account those people employed by themselves who may also (but not necessarily) have full-time paid employees. Those self-employed who have employees, namely, employers, are also included in this indicator.

According to the results compiled by the United Nations (quoted by Weeks and Seiler, 2001), the Rate of Economic Activity for adult women is 40 per cent or higher in most countries in Latin America, from Guatemala's 32 per cent to Jamaica's 69 per cent. Peru has a rate of 55 per cent. The study also indicates that the percentage of women in administrative and managerial positions varies from 10 per cent to 48 per cent in Latin America and the Caribbean. In Peru, 23 per cent of those positions are held by women. The percentage of employers and self-employed persons who are women ranges from 7 per cent in Cuba to 49 per cent in Bolivia. In Peru, this percentage is 42 per cent.

In Latin America, surveys made by the NAWBO from the United States and IBM in Argentina and Mexico, and in Brazil by the Serviço Brasileiro de Apoio às Micro e Pequenas Empresas (SEBRAE), a Brazilian organization devoted to the promotion of entrepreneurship, represent the first attempts at describing the economic and demographic characteristics of women entrepreneurs, but they were not conducted on representative samples (Echeverri-Carroll and Brandazza, 2002). This lack of statistical information and research in Latin America limits the analysis and the generation of the hypothesis for research.

According to Echeverri-Carroll and Brandazza (2002), Latin American women entrepreneurs have certain advantages and disadvantages over those in the United States and Canada. The relative advantages include the availability of domestic help (cheap labour force); close relationships among family members, ensuring child care; and the high urban concentration, thus avoiding long distances between work and home. The relative disadvantages are the separation of the roles of men and women, where women are responsible for child and home care; as well as the low level of entrepreneurial activity in Latin American countries.

Summary

Entrepreneurship has been an expanding area of research in academic circles for the past decades because of the acknowledgment that the creation of new enterprises is related to the economic growth of countries, the generation of employment and market development (Weeks and Seiler, 2001). The special interest in understanding women's entrepreneurial activity is due to their important participation, as well as the evidence that shows that female entrepreneurial activity presents different organizational procedures and styles than those of men. In addition, there is an important and positive relation between the participation of women who are employers or self-employed and the increase in the GDP (NFWBO, quoted by Weeks and Seiler, 2001).

According to the *Global Entrepreneur Monitor: 2004 Report on Women and Entrepreneurship*, carried out by Minniti et al. (2005), entrepreneurial activity plays an important role in the creation of an active and dynamic economy, especially female entrepreneurial activity, whose enterprises throughout the world represent between one-fourth and one-third of the enterprises of the formal economy and, apparently, a more important role in informal sectors.

In the United States, two out of five enterprises (40.2 per cent) are majority-owned by women, with a total of 10.4 million enterprises (2006 estimate) that contribute 1.9 billion dollars in annual sales and employ 12.8 million of people (Center for Women's Business Research, 2006).

Studies show that women find difficulties that are distinct from those that men face in operating and starting an enterprise (Neider, 1987) and their motivations to start an enterprise are different. Hisrich and Brush (1986) show that women entrepreneurs and men entrepreneurs are quite similar in terms of personality and backgrounds, except for the fact that most women are older when they set up the entrepreneurial venture. They differ in other aspects, however, such as their motivations, the processes involved when starting an enterprise, the problems they face and their administrative and entrepreneurial skills.

Minniti et al. (2005) demonstrated that the decision to start a new enterprise is more complex for women than for men, and women tend to be more sensitive than men regarding non-monetary incentives. Other studies show that women start their own enterprises because it is easier to combine their responsibilities at home with those at work. For women, more than for men, the decision to start an enterprise is usually related to economic need or to a flexible schedule or place to reconcile family and work needs (Brush, 1992; Goffee and Scase, 1985).

Research on women entrepreneurs is quite plentiful in developed countries, especially in the United States, Canada and the United Kingdom, while there is not much knowledge about women and their enterprises in Latin America. According to the results of the United Nations (quoted by Weeks and Seiler, 2001), the participation of women in working activities is increasing in Latin America.

The *Global Entrepreneurship Monitor: Peru 2004–2005* report (Serida et al., 2005) points out that the global average of the ratio female TEA/male TEA rate is 0.55, that is, the male TEA is almost twice the female TEA in most countries. In Peru, this ratio is 0.94, the highest value of all the countries included in this study, which indicates that for every enterprising man there is almost one enterprising woman. Peru also has the highest TEA rate: 40.3 per cent for the whole country and 39.1 per cent for women (p. 58). This high index is mainly due to the high levels of unemployment that require men and women to generate new businesses. On the other hand, Peru has the second highest rate of enterprise mortality in Latin America (11.45 per cent) and one of the study's highest ratios of incipient enterprises/growing enterprises (2.43), which could be an indicator of problems for increasing incipient enterprises, a high level of unemployment, a business climate in the country that invites investments or that it has recently created new opportunities for doing business.

According to Weeks and Seiler (2001), upon analysis of the relationship of the economic growth in Latin America and the Caribbean with the economic activity of women in general, it can be seen that promoting their entrepreneurial efforts have an important impact on the economic growth and prosperity of the region.

Conclusions

During recent decades, major efforts have been made all over the world to stimulate the development of entrepreneurial activity as a result of the acknowledgement that enterprise creation is related to economic growth and job generation (Weeks and Seiler, 2001). To be able to understand the entrepreneurship phenomenon, the first step is to explore the backgrounds of entrepreneurs as well as the motivations behind entrepreneurial activity, given that the success of an enterprise depends on the person's initiatives to create a viable business (Mitchell, 2004).

In recent decades, entrepreneurship has been a growing field for research in the world, especially in developed countries (Weeks and Seiler, 2001). However, most knowledge of entrepreneurial activity is based on studies about men entrepreneurs (Brush and Bird, 2002; Hisrich and Brush, 1984; Hisrich and Brush, 1986). Several authors consider that it is inadequate to use the results of studies on men entrepreneurs for the cases of women entrepreneurs, because even if men's and women's entrepreneurial attitudes are influenced by some of the same variables, these factors do not influence both genders in the same way or with the same intensity, and women show organizational processes and styles that are different from those of men (Brush and Bird, 2002; Carter and Cannon, 1992; Minniti et al., 2005; Mitchell, 2004; Weeks and Seiler, 2001; Zapalska, 1997). Besides, most of the knowledge of entrepreneurial activity in general, and especially of women, is from developed countries, while in Latin America little is known about women and their enterprises. This lack of knowledge of entrepreneurial activity in Latin America represents an obstacle to understanding the phenomenon of women entrepreneurs in contexts different from those in developed countries. Cultural differences between Latin America countries and developed countries make the entrepreneurial experiences of Latin America women unique.

It is important to increase knowledge of women's entrepreneurial activity, not only because the number of women-owned enterprises is growing in the world, but also because current evidence shows that women's and men's motivations and profiles may be different (Mitchell, 2004). Increasing the knowledge of women's entrepreneurial activity, in Latin America in particular, will help to understand the phenomenon and facilitate the implementation of support programmes for the creation of enterprises by women and develop a favourable environment for entrepreneurial activity.

References

Aidis, R. (2002). *Why less? The gendered aspects of small- and medium-sized enterprise ownership under economic transition*. Working paper. Retrieved 15 December 2005 from Tinbergen Institute Amsterdam in http://www.tinbergen.nl.

Allen, S. and Truman, C. (1993). *Women in Business: Perspectives on Women Entrepreneurs*. London: Routledge Press.

Baycan, T., Masurel, E. and Nijkamp, P. (2003). *Diversity in entrepreneurship: Ethnic and female roles in urban economic life*. Retrieved 15 December 2003 from Fondazione Eni Enrico Mattei in http://www.feem.it/activ/_wp.html.

Bennett, R. and Dann, S. (2000). The changing experience of Australian female entrepreneurs. *Australian Female Entrepreneurs, 7*(2), 75–83.

Bowen, D. and Hisrich, R. (1986). The female entrepreneurs: A career development perspective. *Academy of Management Review, 11*, 393–407.

Brush, C. (1992). Research on women business owners: Past trends, a new perspective and future directions. *Entrepreneurship Theory and Practice, 16*(4), 5–30.

Brush, C. and Bird, B. (2002). A gendered perspective on organizational creation. *Entrepreneurship Theory and Practice, 26*(3), 41–66.

Cambridge University Press (2008). *Cambridge Advanced Learner's Dictionary*. Retrieved on 2 January 2008 from http://dictionary.cambridge.org.

Carland, J.W., Hoy, F., Boulton, W. and Carland, J.C. (1984). Differentiating entrepreneurs from small business owners: A conceptualization. *Academy of Management Review, 9*(2), 354–359.

Carter, S. and Cannon, T. (1992). *Women as Entrepreneurs*. London: Academic Press.

Center for Women's Business Research. (n.d.). *Top facts about women-owned businesses*. Retrieved 6 October 2006 from http://www.cfwbr.org/facts/index.php.

Center for Women's Business Research. (2006). *Women-owned businesses in the United States 2006*. Retrieved 6 October 2006 from http://www.cfwbr.org/assets/344_2006nationalfactsheet.pdf.

Cooper, A. and Dunkelberg, W. (1981). A new look at business entry. In Vesper, K.H. (Ed.), *Frontiers of entrepreneurship research* (pp. 1–20). Wellesley, MA: Babson College Center for Entrepreneurship.

Dechant, K. and Al Lamky, A. (2005). Toward an understanding of Arab women entrepreneurs in Bahrain and Oman. *Journal of Developmental Entrepreneurship*, 10(2), 123–140.

Echeverri-Carroll, E. and Brandazza, D. (2002). Empresarias decididas, Women entrepreneurs in the Americas. *Texas Business Review*. Retrieved 15 December 2003 from http://www.stexas.edu/depts/bbr/tbr.

Gartner, W. (1985). A conceptual framework for describing the phenomenon of new venture creation. *The Academy of Management Review*, 10(4), 696–706.

Goffee, R. and Scase, R. (1985). *Women in Charge: The Experiences of Female Entrepreneurs*. London: George Allen and Unwin.

Harper, D. (2001). *Online Etymology Dictionary*. Retrieved 2 December 2007 from http://www.etymonline.com/index.php.

HarperCollins (2003). *Collins Cobuild English Dictionary for Advanced Learners (8th ed.)*. Retrieved 2 December 2007 from http://diccionario.reverso.net.

HarperCollins (2005). *Collins Spanish Dictionary (4th edn)*. Retrieved 2 December 2007 from http://diccionario.reverso.net.

Hisrich, R. (1986). The woman entrepreneur: A comparative analysis. *Leadership and Organization Development Journal*, 7(2), 8–16.

Hisrich, R. and Ayse Öztürk, S. (1999). Women entrepreneurs in a developing economy. *Journal of Management Development*, 38(2), 114–124.

Hisrich, R. and Brush, C. (1984). The woman entrepreneur: Management skills and business problems. *Journal of Small Business Management*, 22(1), 30–37.

Hisrich, R. and Brush, C. (1986). *The Woman Entrepreneur: Starting, Financing and Managing a Successful New Business*. Toronto, Canada: Lexington Books, D.C. Heath and Company.

Hisrich, R. and Brush, C. (1991). Antecedent influences on women-owned businesses. *Journal of Management Psychology*, 2(2), 9–16.

Hisrich, R., Brush, C. and Lerner, M. (1997). Israeli women entrepreneurs: An examination of factor affecting performance. *Journal of Business Venturing*, 12(4), 315–350.

Hisrich, R. and Fan, Z. (1991). Women entrepreneurs in the People's Republic of China, an exploratory study. *Journal of Managerial Psychology*, 6(3), 3–12.

Hisrich, R. and Fulop, G. (1994). The role of women entrepreneurs in Hungary's transition economy. *International Studies of Management and Organization*, 24(4), 100–118.

Hisrich, R. and O'Brien, M. (1981). The woman entrepreneur from a business and sociological perspective. In Vesper, K.H. (Ed.), *Frontiers on Entrepreneurship Research* (pp. 21–39). Wellesley, MA: Babson College Center for Entrepreneurship.

Hisrich, R. and O'Brien, M. (1982). The woman entrepreneur as a reflection of the type of business. In Vesper, K.H. (Ed.), *Frontiers of Entrepreneurship Research* (pp. 54–67). Wellesley, MA: Babson College Center for Entrepreneurship.

Inman, K. (2000). *Women's Resources in Business Start-up, A Study of Black and White Women Entrepreneurs*. New York: Garland Publishing.

Izyumov, A. and Razumnova, I. (2000). Women entrepreneurs in Russia: Learning to survive the market. *Journal of Developmental Entrepreneurship*, 5(1), 1–19.

Landstrom, H. (1999). The roots of entrepreneurship research. *New England Journal of Entrepreneurship*, 2(2), 9–21.

Langan-Fox, J. and Roth, S. (1995). Achievement motivation and female entrepreneurs. *Journal of Occupational and Organizational Psychology*, 3(68), 209–218.

Lee, J. (1996). The motivation of women entrepreneurs in Singapore. *Women in Management Review*, 11(2), 18–29.

Lee-Gosselin, H. and Grisé, J. (1990). Are women owner-managers challenging our definitions of entrepreneurship? An in-depth survey. *Journal of Business Ethics*, 9(4), 423–433.

Mattis, M. (2004). Women entrepreneurs: Out from under the glass ceiling. *Women in Management Review*, 19(3), 154–163.

Ministerio de Industria, Turismo, Integración y Negociaciones Comerciales Internacionales. (1997). *Desarrollando la Perspectiva de Género en los Centros de Servicio Empresarial [Developing a Gender Perspective in the Centers of Business Services]*. Lima, Perú: Fondo para la equidad del género, DESIDE, COSUDE.

Minniti, M., Arenius, P. and Langowitz, N. (2005). *Global entrepreneurship monitor: 2004 report on women and entrepreneurship*. Retrieved on 10 January 2006 from http://www.gemconsortium.org//download.asp?id=478.

Mitchell, B. (2004). Motives of entrepreneurs: A case study of South Africa. *The Journal of Entrepreneurship*, 13(2), 167–193.

Mitra, R. (2002). The growth pattern of women-run enterprises: An empirical study in India. *Journal of Development Entrepreneurship*, 7(2), 217–237.

Moore, D. and Buttner, E. (1997). *Women Entrepreneurs: Moving Beyond the Glass Ceiling*. Thousand Oaks, CA: Sage Publications.

Mroczkowski, T. (1997). Women as employees and entrepreneurs in the Polish transformation. *Industrial Relations Journal, 28*(2), 83–91.

Neider, L. (1987). A preliminary investigation of female entrepreneurs in Florida. *Journal of Small Business Management, 25*(3), 22–28.

Orhan, M. and Scott, D. (2001). Why women enter into entrepreneurship: An exploratory model. *Journal of Management Review, 16*(5/6), 232–242.

Oxford University Press (1998). *Dictionary of Sociology (2nd edn)*. Retrieved 2 December 2007 from http://www.oup.co.uk/.

Pardo, L. and Gómez, J. (1990). El perfil de la mujer empresaria y las razones de éxito o fracaso en su gestión *[Profile of women entrepreneurs and the reasons for success or failure in their administration]*. *JE. Academia Revista Latinoamericana de Administración, 1*(5), 73–99.

Real Academia Española (2001). *Diccionario de la Lengua Española [Dictionary of Spanish Language] (22nd edn)*. Retrieved 2 January 2008 from http://www.rae.es.

Sarri, K. and Trihopoulou, A. (2005). Female entrepreneurs' personal characteristics and motivation: A review of the Greek situation. *Women in Management Review, 20*(1/2) 24–36.

Scheinberg, S. and MacMillan, I. (1988). An 11 country study of motivations to start a business. In Kirchhoff, B., Long, W., McMillan, W., Vesper, K. and Wetzel, W. (Eds), *Frontiers of entrepreneurship research* (pp. 669–687). Wellesley, MA: Babson College Center for Entrepreneurial Studies.

Schindehutte, M., Morris, M. and Brennan, C. (2003). Entrepreneurs and motherhood: Impacts on their children in South Africa and the United States. *Journal of Small Business Management, 41*(1), 94–107.

Schumpeter, J. (1934). *The Theory of Economic Development*. Translated by R. Opie. Cambridge: Harvard University Press.

Schwartz, E. (1976). Entrepreneurship: A new female frontier. *Journal of Contemporary Business, 5*(1), 47–76.

Serida, J., Borda, A., Nakamatsu, K., Morales, O. and Yamakama, P. (2005). *Global entrepreneurship monitor: Peru 2004–2005*. Lima, Perú: Ediciones ESAN.

Siew Kim, J. and Seow Ling, C. (2001). Work-family conflict of women entrepreneurs in Singapore. *Women in Management Review, 16*(5/6), 204–221.

Smith-Hunter, A. (2003). *Diversity and Entrepreneurship*. New York: University Press of America.

The National Foundation for Women Business Owners (NFWBO). (2000). *Las mujeres empresarias: Una fuente de crecimiento económico [Businesswomen: a source of economic development]*. Retrieved 20 November 2006 from http://www.nfwbo.org.

United States Agency of International Development. (2005). *Diagnóstico y Recomendaciones para Mejorar los Programas y Servicios de Apoyo a las Micro, Pequeñas y Medianas Empresas (MIPYMEs) en el Perú [Diagnosis and Suggestions to Improve the Support Programs and Services to Micro, Small and Middle Enterprises (MYPYMEs) in Peru]*. Lima, Perú: Proyecto Crecer.

Voeten, J. (2002a). *Criteria to define women entrepreneurs who own and manage micro and small enterprises: Working paper 1 in the framework of the project "Training for women in micro and small enterprises, phase 2 (TWMSE2)"*. Maastricht, The Netherlands: Maastricht School of Management.

Voeten, J. (2002b). *Management training effects on women entrepreneurs who own and manage micro and small enterprises: Working paper 3 in the framework of the project "Training for Women in Micro and Small Enterprises, phase 2 (TWMSE2)"*. Maastricht, The Netherlands: Maastricht School of Management.

Weeks, J. and Seiler, D. (2001). *Women's entrepreneurship in Latin America: An exploration of current knowledge*. Retrieved 10 December 2003 from Inter-American Development Bank from web: http://www.iadb.org/publications/.

Zapalska, A. (1997). A profile of woman entrepreneurs and enterprises in Poland. *Journal of Small Business Management*, 35(4), 76–82.

2

Female Entrepreneurship: Why do Women Become Entrepreneurs?

Theoretical Background

In order to obtain information and knowledge on women entrepreneurs, the first step is to understand the motivations that drive entrepreneurial activity. To understand or stimulate entrepreneurship, the first things to learn are the factors that motivate a person to start a career as an entrepreneur (Kantis et al., 2002; Mitchell, 2004). Looking at the factors that motivate women, one sees that it is important to stimulate entrepreneurial activity because the success of a small enterprise depends on the initiatives of a person to create a viable business (Mitchell, 2004).

According to Cooper (1981), the decision to start an enterprise seems to be influenced by three main factors: (a) the entrepreneur's background, including the different aspects that have an impact on their motivations and perceptions, such as their knowledge and skills; (b) the nature of the organization they have previously worked in, which influence the location, nature and the paths of new enterprises; and (c) the factors that generate a climate more or less favourable for founding a new enterprise. The entrepreneur's background includes psychological characteristics (the need for achievement and the conviction that they can control their own destinies) and several family aspects (father or some close relative is owner of his/her own enterprise), the type of education received, and professional experience. The nature of the organization for which they have previously worked influences the nature of the skills and knowledge gained by the entrepreneur in her previous working experience, the prior contacts obtained that can be associated with their new enterprise, the motivations or frustrations in the work field that can influence the person to be oriented towards independent activity, and the geographical location of the enterprise.

Research shows that most entrepreneurs start their enterprises where they are already located, and the nature of their business is generally derived from the organizational nature of their previous job. Factors that generate a climate more or less favourable for the formation of new enterprises include the availability of risk capital, economic conditions, another entrepreneur who acts as a model or advisor, the availability of personnel and support services and access to customers.

In a study performed in Latin American and East Asian countries (Kantis et al., 2002), it was found that in both groups, the main motivation for people to become entrepreneurs is the need for personal development and the desire to become their own boss.

The literature presents a wide range of possible motivations for women. An initial study (Schwartz, 1976) of 20 women entrepreneurs in the United States identified as the main motivations for starting a business: the need for achievement, for independence, for a higher work satisfaction and for economic needs. Some studies have found that women start their own business because it is easier for them to combine their family responsibilities with work (Goffee and Scase, 1985; Brush, 1992).

Goffee and Scase (1985) obtained qualitative information of 54 women from the United Kingdom to develop a typology of women entrepreneurs based on two dimensions: the degree to which women were capable of accepting traditional gender roles and the degree to which they had the ideal of becoming entrepreneurs. They identified four types of women entrepreneurs: *conventional, innovative, domestic* and *radical. Conventional* women entrepreneurs highly value their traditional gender roles and their ideals as an entrepreneur. These women usually have fragmented job histories and were forced into self-employment by economic needs. Their income complements the family income, minimizing the growth of the enterprise in order to reconcile their family and working roles, and in hopes that their enterprises do not interfere with their domestic responsibilities. *Innovative* women entrepreneurs have strong entrepreneurial ideals, but with little attachment to traditional roles. These women are usually highly educated and committed to their enterprises, thus restricting their social lives often; they are motivated by the achievement of their goals; many have achieved success in their careers, but they have chosen self-employment as a reaction to feeling that their professional perspectives are restricted. They are seen as "self-made" women in a world in which men are dominant. *Domestic* women entrepreneurs have little attachment to entrepreneurial ideals, but are convinced of their traditional roles as women. These women prioritize their domestic responsibilities and have a high level of commitment to their families; they became entrepreneurs for autonomy or personal satisfaction more than for economic reasons, usually using some kind of personal talent. *Radical* entrepreneurs are women frequently involved in enterprises, politicians by nature, with little attachment to entrepreneurial ideals or traditional gender roles. These women become entrepreneurs as a way of improving their place in society and are usually considered feminists. They are not motivated by money but by gaining autonomy and freedom from the influence of men.

Carter and Cannon (1992) criticized the Goffee and Scase typology because they believed that these categorization factors were not appropriate for an analysis of the behaviour of women entrepreneurs, and also, that women's entrepreneurial experience changes with the stages of their life cycle. They studied 60 women enterprise owners in London and identified five ideal types. They formulated a hypothesis that the differences among women entrepreneurs were behavioural and motivational factors, their desire to start an enterprise, and that these factors influence their process of change. They identified the following types of women entrepreneurs: (a) *wandering*, typically young women that try self-employment in response to their economic needs; (b) *aspiring*, women with a high level of education who use training as a way to compensate their limited working experience; (c) *winners*, comparatively older women who have had relevant working experience; (d) *returning ones*, women who choose self-employment as a way of returning to economic activity after a pause in their careers; and (e) *traditionalists*, women 45 years or older who have always worked in family enterprises.

Hisrich and Brush (1986) studied women entrepreneurs in the United States and found that the most common reasons for starting enterprises were work frustration, being unemployed, boredom or widowhood. The main motivations were the need for independence, work satisfaction, need for achievement, money, status, power, economic needs and job security. "In other words, women entrepreneurs tend to be more interested in self-fulfillment than in money and power" (p. 30).

Lee-Gosselin and Grisé (1990) studied 400 women entrepreneurs in Quebec and found that in more than half of the enterprises (54 per cent), the idea of starting it had come from themselves (an old dream, the desire to use their own talents, to be acknowledged by others, logical extension of working experience, the need to control their own lives). Many women recognized an opportunity (21 per cent) and others were influenced by people close to them. "Most of these motives express an entrepreneurial characteristic: self-determination" (Lee-Gosselin and Grisé, 1990, p. 425).

Lee-Gosselin and Grisé (1990) analysed the motives for starting an enterprise: updating themselves, use of their own talents, economic needs, have something of their own, have something they can control and through which they can express themselves, create job positions for their families, improve the quality of their lives because work is too demanding and constraining for their role as a mother. Their reasons are very interesting because they express the interdependence of the different roles women play; that starting an enterprise can be the answer to the demands generated by their roles as mother and wife/partner, or the lack of control women experience in their lives. The above-mentioned authors concluded that:

> It seems that for many of these women, to start a business is a way to create their own employment, an instrument for personal development and a flexible response to their economic and professional needs, while adapting to their family responsibilities. We also observed that for some women entrepreneurs, being an owner-manager is an extension of her parent and spouse/partner roles, and it is instrumental to these dominant roles in her socialization. (p. 431)

Lee (1996) analysed women's motivations in Singapore using the theory of need as the theoretical framework, and concluded that women are motivated by a high need for achievement, a medium need for domination and moderate need for affiliation and autonomy. Orhan and Scott (2001) analysed 25 women entrepreneurs in France and created a consolidated model of entrepreneurial motivation, in which they identified seven motives for women to become entrepreneurs. The categories are: agreed dynasty, without an alternative, entrepreneurship by chance, natural succession, forced entrepreneurship, informed entrepreneur and pure entrepreneur.

Buttner and Moore (1997) analysed the reasons why 129 executives in the United States left their professional careers to become entrepreneurs and how they measure their success. They found that motivations are complex and usually are a combination of personal aspirations and organizational influence.

Their main motives were the chance to face challenges, self-determination and their desire to balance family and working responsibilities. Through entrepreneurship, these women found the opportunity to develop their skills, use their experience and have the freedom to control their lives (Buttner and Moore, 1997). The study divides women entrepreneurs in two groups: *intentional entrepreneurs* and *corporative climbers*. The first are women who have always wanted to have their own enterprise but first, worked for others to gain experience. The second ones are women who tried to have corporative careers, but they left them behind due to negative factors at work or to take advantage of an entrepreneurial opportunity.

Inman (2000) carried out studies on the cases of 61 women entrepreneurs in the United States on the basis of two main questions: what motivates women to start their enterprises and, after they have decided to be proprietors, how they obtain the resources to achieve their entrepreneurial goals? He found that women face contradictory barriers and goals in their personal and working life. He also found that:

> *Women's increased independence from men means that men provide less financial support to their families than women do, making women's job earnings necessary for their own and their children's support. Higher divorce rates mean more women are single mothers, a status fraught with conflicting pushes and pulls between job and family. Increased living costs frequently makes second incomes for married couples a necessity, not a luxury ... Self-employment, while increasingly an option for women, is not without contradictory choices and goals as well. Women choose to start a business under many different circumstances for many reasons, sometimes voluntarily and sometimes involuntarily. While some women may pursue a career or trade that naturally leads them into business ownership, others are forced or nudged out of paid employment by recession, restructuring, or discrimination. (p. 5)*

Echeverri-Carroll and Brandazza (2002) consider that women tend to be pushed to becoming entrepreneurs by the negative aspects of the corporative working environment, such as the limitations of the glass ceiling, other factors of discrimination and inflexible hours. Research shows that the potential for increased income as self-employed and the demand of flexible hours push women to create their own enterprises. The possibility of creating their own working schedule lets them find a better balance for their professional and family responsibilities.

According to the study conducted by Echeverri-Carroll and Brandazza (2000), data for the United States show that most self-employed women are married and that their husbands may also be self-employed and also have insurance covering the whole family. Women who have never been married only represent 7.3 per cent of all their case studies of self-employed women for the period 1975–1990; married women (still living with the husband) represent 75 per cent of the self-employed during the same period.

Kuiper (quoted by Mitchell, 2004) studied women entrepreneurs in Africa and indicates that the factors that motivate African women to become entrepreneurs are family circumstances, economic pressure, the urge for being economically dependent, a change in their lives and the need to improve their economic condition. Mitchell (2004) studied men's and women's motivations to become entrepreneurs in South Africa and found that both men and women entrepreneurs have as their main motives the need for independence, for material incentives and achievement. Men entrepreneurs, compared to women entrepreneurs, were more motivated by the need to offer security for their families and wanting to make a change with their enterprises. Women entrepreneurs were more motivated by the need for continuous learning and obtaining more money to survive.

Circumstances and Motives to Become an Entrepreneur

The literature does not make a clear difference between circumstances and motives for women to become entrepreneurs. *Circumstances* are defined as *all that is around someone* (Real Academia Española, 2001) and refer to "the situations or events that, when they happen in a certain context, drive women to become entrepreneurs" (Avolio, 2010). An event is defined as *something that happens, especially when it is of some importance* (Real Academia Española, 2001) and it refers to the objective facts that affect women's decision to become entrepreneurs, such as the death of the father in a family enterprise, or the loss of an dependent job (Avolio, 2010). *Situation* is defined as *the disposition of something regarding the place they hold* (Real Academia Española, 2001) and it refers to the factors that influence women's decision to become entrepreneurs and that depend on their own perception, such as their dissatisfaction regarding family income or their lack of professional growth perspective (Avolio, 2010).

Motives, in turn, are defined as "the construct that represents a force in the brain, a force which organizes perception, intellection and action in such a way as to transform an unsatisfying situation and increases satisfaction" (Murray, 1938, p. 124). In other words, in the presence of a gap between the current situation and the desired one, individuals are moved by an internal force that makes them establish a conduct that will allow them to reach the state they desire. It is worth mentioning that in social motives classification, the terms *motive* and *need* are used are used interchangeably. In this context, McClelland and Atkinson call them social motives in their study, while Maslow refers to the hierarchy of human needs (Fernández-Abascal, 2001).

Motives can be divided into primary and secondary motives. Primary motives are biological, and secondary motives derive from tensions generated by an external situation. Additionally, primary ones are related to physical satisfaction, while secondary ones are related to emotional or mental satisfaction (Murray, 1938). Murray (1938) identified 20 needs or manifest motives, that is, motives that have a direct influence on behaviour. Steers and Braunstein (1976) developed an instrument (Manifest Needs Questionnaire) intended to measure four motives: achievement, power, affiliation and autonomy, because the literature shows that these four have an influence in working attitudes and behaviour. Such authors found that commitment to the organization one works for is positively related with the need for affiliation and achievement, and inversely with the need for autonomy. Thus, people with high *achievement motive* and those with high *affiliation motive* see the organization they work in as the means to satisfy their needs. Someone with high achievement motive will be influenced by the chances, goals and performance they can achieve, while someone with high affiliation motive will be influenced by working relations they may establish.

The need for achievement is related to compliance with a task that entails some degree of difficulty, and that implies that it has to be done quickly and independently, in addition to overcoming obstacles and reaching a standard of excellence (Murray, 1938, p. 164). The need to reach excellence motivates the individual to overcome obstacles, to fight to comply with difficult tasks as well and as quickly as possible (Murray, 1938) and to do something better than it was done before (McClelland, 1974). From the aforementioned, it could be said that, occasionally, people with high motive for achievement tend to get involved in activities with the sole purpose of discovering whether they are able to do it successfully (Lang and Fries, 2006). According to McClelland, someone with a high need for achievement is characterized by their perseverance, by assuming calculated risks and by actively looking for success in their performance. They are enterprising and innovative people who perform better in challenging tasks or tasks that have an intrinsic motivation. They also assume responsibility for their conduct and they are interested in receiving feedback on their performance (Fernández-Abascal, 2001; Reeve, 1994).

The *motive of power* is the need to control the feelings and behaviour of others; is the desire of exercising influence upon others through suggestion, seduction, persuasion or order; it consists of persuading others to act as you want or need (Murray, 1938, p. 152). The need for power is expressed through the desire for status, to have an active leadership role in groups, to organize and direct other people's activities. Studies show that entrepreneurial activity presents a need for power since the entrepreneur is the highest authority in the enterprise (Lee, 1996).

The *motive of affiliation* implies the need to establish cooperative and reciprocal connections, as well as the desire to win the affection of significant person (Murray, 1938, p. 174). They are people who need to interact with others and, generally, they are very anxious for those relationships. They fear disapproval from others and they try very hard to find security in other people. However, among the positive characteristics of the *motive of affiliation*, we can mention the concern of these people with the quality of their social relationships, as well as their desire of being involved in warm, close and positive relationships (Reeve, 1994, p. 280).

The need for *autonomy* is related to the desire to be independent and act according to one's own free will, without being subject to the pressure or coercion of an authority or others in general (Murray, 1938, p. 156). In comparison with the stable job, entrepreneurship offers the individuals a higher level of freedom to direct their work and personal lives (Lee, 1996).

Why do Women Become Entrepreneurs?

A qualitative approach of multiple case studies under a holistic design was used by Avolio (2010) to explore the motives of women entrepreneurs. Case study was chosen as the appropriate strategy because it allows performing an in-depth study to obtain knowledge about complex, sensitive and personal matters such as women's decisions to become entrepreneurs.

The cases were rigorously chosen to reflect the diversity of situations experienced by women entrepreneurs, considering the following dimensions:

age, civil status, educational level, the way ownership was obtained, length of operation and the economic sector and size of the enterprise. The data was collected primarily through in-depth interviews of approximately 90 minutes during several sessions and in several places (mainly in their enterprises, but also in their homes or in public places). The interviews were open, followed a guideline, recorded and then transcribed. Additionally, notes and photographs were taken before the interviews, as well as during them, with comments and perceptions of the researcher recorded to capture the particular aspects of the entrepreneurs and to analyse each case. The information was coded, categorized and analysed using analytic induction (Strauss and Corbin, 1998).

The information was analysed according to the six phases suggested by Marshall and Rossman (1999): organize and prepare the information for the analysis; generate categories, topics and patterns through a thorough review of the information; code the categories and the topics, marking the quotes in the information; test the initial findings; look for alternative explanations for the information; and write the report. The information was processed in the *Atlas.ti* version 5.2. in order to maintain clear evidence of the narratives, the information codification and the conclusions.

POPULATION AND SAMPLE SELECTION

The study presented in this chapter was conducted in Metropolitan Lima, Peru. Peru is a particularly interesting context for research on entrepreneurship. Peru has the highest Female Total Entrepreneurial Activity (TEA) rate in the world (39.1 per cent), according to the *Global Entrepreneurship Monitor: 2004 Report on Women and Entrepreneurship* (GEM) study carried out on 34 countries by Minniti et al. (2005) for Babson's College Center for Women's Leadership, in the United States. It has also the highest TEA rate (40.3 per cent) registered by the GEM study since its creation in 2000 (Serida et al., 2005, p. 21). 50.1 per cent of the Peruvian population (National Institute of Statistics and Computer Sciences (INEI), 2006b) and 21.4 per cent of the heads of household are women (INEI, 2006a). In 1981, only 26 out of every 100 Peruvian women of working age were currently working, representing 24.6 per cent of the Economically Active Population (EAP) (Blondet and Montero, 1994, p. 207); and this number increased to 61 out of every 100 by the year 2004, increasing to 43.8 per cent participation by women in the country's economic activity (INEI, 2005a, p. 273).

These data show the importance of women's entrepreneurial activity in Peru, a situation similar to what happens in other countries of Latin America and the world. However in Latin America, and especially in Peru, there are very few studies about the phenomenon of women entrepreneurs.

The population of entrepreneurs includes those women who own 50 per cent or more of a formal enterprise (regardless of the way they obtained ownership), are actively involved in their operation as managers or administrators and generate employment for themselves and other people.

To operationalize the definition of entrepreneur, we divided it into eight criteria used in previous studies: (a) to have an enterprise operating formally, to consider only formal businesses; (b) to have 50 per cent or more ownership of the business (shares, voting participation or entrepreneurial activity as an individual), regardless of the way the ownership was obtained; (c) to have more than two employees, in order to distinguish entrepreneurship from self-employment; (d) to have at least two years of formal operation, in order to distinguish short-term opportunities from a long-term commitment to the business; (e) to have an important administrative role in the enterprise; (f) to work full time in the enterprise; (g) to receive the majority of one's income from the enterprise; and (h) to be linked with the enterprise for a minimum of two years. Specific questions were prepared for each of these criteria, and only those women who met the criteria were chosen to participate in the study (Bennett and Dann, 2000; Inman, 2000; Lee-Gosselin and Grisé, 1990; Voeten, 2002).

As this is a qualitative study, it does not use probability sampling or convenience sampling; it is based, rather, on a *purposeful sampling* (Maxwell, 1996, p. 70). The *purposeful sampling* has the following objectives for the study: to achieve representativeness and identify cases of women entrepreneurs; to adequately capture the heterogeneity of the population of women entrepreneurs in order to make sure that the conclusions adequately represent the diverse ranges of probabilities (*maximum variation sample*); and to examine the cases that are critical for the theories considered or that will be developed in the study (Maxwell, 1996, pp. 71–72). The sample was built using a combination of *snowball* and *maximum variation* techniques.

To identify potential participants, sources were used to build the sample, such as women entrepreneurs who have applied for loans in banks that specialize in microenterprises and small enterprises, newspaper articles about women entrepreneurs and business organizations and later, referrals from the entrepreneurs themselves. Each one was required to fulfil the eight criteria that define an entrepreneur in order to be included in the sample. The cases were rigorously chosen to reflect the diversity of situations experienced by women entrepreneurs, taking into consideration age, civil status, educational level, the enterprise's economic sector, how ownership was obtained, the time the business has been in operation and the size of the enterprise.

To answer the research questions adequately, 24 cases were selected, which made it possible to obtain enough information to carry out a transversal analysis of the cases and respond to the research questions. The number of cases selected was based on the theoretical saturation, that is, the point at which incremental learning from the case is minimal because researchers do not obtain any additional knowledge (Glaser and Strauss, 1967). Table 2.1 shows the profiles of the informants.

SOURCES OF EVIDENCE

Three sources of evidence were used for the collection of information: direct observation, in-depth interviews and documentation. The information triangulation technique was used to ensure that conclusions were based on multiple sources of evidence.

The first approach to women entrepreneurs was through direct observation. The researcher carried out field visits to obtain initial knowledge of the women while they were operating their businesses and the nature of their enterprises. The main source of information was the in-depth interviews.

Women were initially contacted by telephone. Three attempts were made to contact someone before excluding them. The researcher presented the study and if the person was interested, the researcher described the study in detail and explained the need to carry out an interview, trying not to affect the entrepreneur's working activity. The most convenient date and place for the interview were agreed upon. During the telephone contact, classification questions were made to establish that the person complied with the criteria of the definition of entrepreneur. Three cases were discarded at the beginning of the personal interview because they did not comply with the classification questions. However, as they had already been visited, an in-depth conversation was held with these women to understand the problems of a woman entrepreneur. Such cases were not valid for the study, but helped to widen the criteria for the research.

Table 2.1   Profiles of informants

	Place of birth	Age	Educational level	Children	Current marital status	Business sectors	How did you come to own the enterprise?	Years the enterprise operates	Number of employees
A	Arequipa	45	Complete High School	3	Partnered	Restaurant	Foundation	6	3
B	Moyobamba	30	Complete Technical Education	1	Married	Hair salon	Foundation	4	8
C	Lima	47	Complete University Education	2	Married	Jewellery production and sale	Foundation	6	4
D	Áncash	57	Incomplete Primary School	3	Married	Consumer products	Foundation	15	8
E	Piura	42	Complete Technical Education	3	Partnered	Hairdresser salon	Foundation	2	5
F	Arequipa	52	Incomplete High school	5	Married	Dressmaking	Foundation	2	10
G	Apurímac	51	Incomplete Technical Education	3	Married	Bakery	Foundation	15	5
H	Lima	50	Incomplete University	2	Married	Sale of plants	Foundation	9	5
I	Lima	44	Complete University Education	4	Married	Building	Foundation	14	45
J	Lima	58	Complete Primary School	4	Married	Sale of fabric and derivatives	Foundation	10	7
K	Lima	20	Incomplete Technical Education	0	Single	Textile design and printing	Heritage	6	11
L	Lima	37	Complete Technical	3	Married	Education	Foundation	4	10

	Place of birth	Age	Educational level	Children	Current marital status	Business sectors	How did you come to own the enterprise?	Years the enterprise operates	Number of employees
M	Arequipa	40	Complete University Education	0	Single	Early childhood education	Foundation	14	15
N	Lima	40	Complete Technical Education	2	Married	Hair salon	Purchase	5	18
O	Italy	71	Complete Technical Education	2	Widow	Pizza parlour	Foundation	29	20
P	Lima	40	Complete Technical Education	2	Married	Sale of machine parts	Foundation	12	14
Q	Ica	42	Complete University Education	0	Divorced	Dental clinic	Foundation	16	25
R	Lima	33	Complete Technical Education	1	Single	Event assistance and production of metal parts	Foundation	11	9
S	Lima	54	Complete Technical Education	2	Married	Travels agency	Foundation	23	200
T	Puno	47	Complete High School	3	Single	Production and sale of handicrafts	Foundation	11	30
U	Lima	42	Complete University Education	2	Divorced	Vehicle sales	Inheritance	56	180
V	Lima	43	Complete High School	3	Married	Shoe sales	Foundation	17	20
W	Lima	45	Complete University Education	3	Married	Hardware sales	Purchase from a relative	7	4
X	Lima	47	Master's Degree	3	Married	Recreation	Foundation	12	120

The objective of the interviews was to capture the motivations of women to become entrepreneurs. Therefore it was essential to generate trust and a sense of cooperation for the interviewees to disclose the required information. The interviews were carried out according to the case protocol. To ensure a relaxed and comfortable process, the interviewees were requested to suggest the place and time that was most convenient for them. Most of the interviews were carried out in work places or homes. Several interviews were carried out in multiple sessions, with an average time of two hours for the first interview and one hour for the second. The second interview was aimed at deepening and specifying details that were not dealt with during the first one.

The interview guide is based on ideas from studies made in Turkey (Hisrich and Ayse Öztürk, 1999), Hungary (Hisrich and Fulop, 1994), Poland (Zapalska, 1987), Singapore (Lee, 1996), the United States (Buttner and Moore, 1997; Hisrich and Brush, 1986, 1991; Hisrich and O'Brien, 1981, 1982; Inman, 2000; Neider, 1987), Canada (Lee-Gosselin and Grisé, 1990) and China (Hisrich and Fan, 1991).

ANALYSIS

A descriptive framework was used to organize the case as a general strategy for the analysis. In order to identify patterns and draw conclusions, a transversal analysis of the cases was used as a specific strategy. The qualitative information was coded, categorized and analysed using analytic induction (Strauss and Corbin, 1998) and procedures suggested by Miles and Huberman (1994) to analyse qualitative information. For the analysis of the information, the steps indicated by Strauss and Corbin (1998) have been followed: open coding (through the identification of concepts, their properties and dimensions), axial coding (relating categories at the level of properties and dimensions) and selective coding (through the integration and refining of the theory).

Following Eisenhardt (1989), the cases were analysed from different perspectives: (a) the identification of demographic, work, educational and family backgrounds; administrative and managerial skills of women entrepreneurs; and the characteristics of the business; and (b) assigning codes for each category, establishing differences and similarities for each of them to identify variations in opportunities and circumstances experienced by women entrepreneurs according to their backgrounds. This first part of the analysis concluded that women can be differentiated according to the life cycle stage at which they become entrepreneurs. Factors and circumstances that stimulated women to become entrepreneurs were then identified. The information was coded according to a provisional list, which was created on the basis of research questions and the conceptual framework used in the study. Other codes were generated using the inductive approach suggested by Eisenhardt (1989) and arose from the knowledge provided by the interviewees. These factors were grouped into categories that showed the diversity of circumstances and motives that led women to become entrepreneurs.

The previous steps were then combined in order to understand the extent to which the backgrounds of women entrepreneurs affect the factors that stimulate them to become entrepreneurs and in which phase of their life cycle they make this decision. This analysis identified how demographic, work, educational and family backgrounds of women entrepreneurs vary according to the circumstances in which women start their businesses and their motivations to become entrepreneurs. As a result, a conceptual framework was proposed to explain why women choose entrepreneurship. Finally, a typology of women entrepreneurs in Peru was developed, according to the life cycle phase during which they chose entrepreneurship and the circumstances and motives that stimulated them to decide to pursue the entrepreneurial activity.

VALIDITY AND RELIABILITY

To develop a high-quality case study, four conditions related with the design of the study must be maximized: *construct validity, internal validity, external validity* and *reliability* (Yin, 2003, p. 19). To ensure these conditions, the strategies suggested by Yin (2003), Creswell (2003), and Maxwell (1996) have been used.

The following strategies were used to ensure *construct validity*: (a) triangulation of the information; (b) key informants revised the draft reports of the cases studied; (c) a chain of evidence was maintained in the analysis; (d) the researcher's bias was clearly specified (Creswell, 2003, p. 196); (e) quasi-statistics were carried out to analyse the information related to each particular conclusion (Maxwell, 1996, p. 95); and (f) two pilot cases were carried out (Feng, 2005, p. 42).

To ensure *internal validity*, the pattern matching strategy was used; patterns emerging from the comparison of cases provided the bases to establish the conclusions of the research. *External validity* establishes the extent to which study findings can be generalized. While quantitative research is based on statistical generalizations, case studies are based on analytic generalization

(Yin, 2003). This study used a conceptual framework as a guide to collect and analyse information. The adopted model is a modified version of Orhan and Scott (2001) regarding the motivations of women to become entrepreneurs. This conceptual framework has been analysed under the *replication logic* in the different cases.

Four strategies have been used in the research to ensure *reliability*. First, the use of a protocol case in which the field procedures are established, including similar procedures for the interviews, techniques to create an atmosphere of trust with the interviewee, forms for observation and interview notes, time of the interview, and so on. Second, the use of a database of each case, with a standardized structure to transfer data and have a solid, complete and detailed register of the information collected. Third, the use of two research assistants in the collection of information who are especially trained for the study and with knowledge of qualitative research methods. Fourth, the use of an external researcher to verify the contents and logic of the information analysis and to compare the conclusions with the ones the researcher considered to be those emerging from the information.

Factors in Becoming Entrepreneurs

Women are influenced by a series of factors when it comes to their decisions to become entrepreneurs. The factors regarding the decision of the women to become entrepreneurs can be grouped into two categories: circumstances and motives, to differentiate those factors of extrinsic origin from those of intrinsic origin to the women entrepreneurs. The motives identified in previous literature do not make a clear distinction between circumstances and personal motives that influence women to choose entrepreneurship.

The circumstances identified refer to events or situations that motivated these women to become entrepreneurs. These circumstances can be objective happenings (such as the death of the father in a family enterprise or the loss of a dependent job) or situations that influence entrepreneurship according to the woman's perception (such as dissatisfaction with the family income or the lack of prospects for professional growth).

Women are influenced to choose entrepreneurship by economic, work, family and personal circumstances. Economic circumstances are economic needs or dissatisfaction with the family income (Table 2.2). Work circumstances are difficulty in finding work because of a lack of skills that restrict opportunities in the labour market, old age or lack of education, lack of prospects for professional growth, frustration with work for economic reasons or consideration of entrepreneurship as the logical continuation of professional growth (Table 2.3). Family circumstances are when entrepreneurship is the way to play their family role or through voluntary family succession, whether the result of opportunity or need (Table 2.4). Personal circumstances are an entrepreneurial role model for the woman, relatives who motivate and support entrepreneurship, personal dissatisfaction or a specific opportunity (Table 2.5).

Motives are defined as "the construct that represents a force in the brain that organizes perception, understanding and behaviour in such a way that it changes a dissatisfactory situation and increases satisfaction" (Murray, 1938, p. 24). The motives expressed by the women for their decision to become entrepreneurs are related to achievement, autonomy, power and affiliation (Table 2.6). Throughout Tables 2.2 to 2.6 the conceptualization of the circumstances and motives identified in the study are presented.

Table 2.2   Economic circumstances identified in women entrepreneurs

Circumstances	Definition
Economic: Basic economic need	When the woman is the only or main person responsible for the family economy and has no other alternative than to become an entrepreneur to sustain the family. The woman created her enterprise only to gain money. Having the major or sole economic responsibility in the household makes the woman turn to entrepreneurial activity to obtain income.
Economic: Dissatisfaction with the family income	When the woman chooses to become an entrepreneur because the family income is not enough to generate savings, develop economically, give better opportunities to her children, have funds for entertainment and give a better quality of life to the woman and her family, even if such income can cover the basic household expenses.

The origin of circumstances influencing entrepreneurship are extrinsic to the woman and are related to external situations that can influence them in a positive or negative way towards entrepreneurship; while the origin of motives that influence entrepreneurship are intrinsic to the woman. The motives tend to persist over time, while circumstances are modified according to the women's experiences.

Table 2.3   Work circumstances identified in women entrepreneurs

Circumstances	Definition
Work: Difficulty to find a job due to lack of opportunities in the labour market	When the woman chooses entrepreneurship because of a lack of opportunities in the labour market. This lack of opportunity is not related to the skills, age or education of the woman, but to external aspects such as the economic or political situation.
Work: difficulty to find a job because of lack of skills	When the woman tries, but does not succeed, in finding a job because she lacks skills required by the labour market.
Work: Difficulty to find job due to old age	When the woman tries to find a job, but does not succeed because of her age and there is no demand for people her age.
Work: Difficulty to find a job due to insufficient education	When the woman tries to find a job, but does not succeed due to a lack of adequate training required by the labour market.
Work: Lack of prospects of professional growth	When the woman employee has little chance of being promoted in her job, and this generates personal frustration.
Work: Frustration for economic reasons	When the woman employee believes she is being inadequately paid in her job, generating personal frustration.
Work: Dissatisfied with a male-dominated work environment	When the woman is dissatisfied with the existence of a male-dominated work environment, in which she is not offered the same conditions as men.
Work: Logical continuation of professional growth	When women employees believe entrepreneurship to be the logical next step in their professional growth.

Table 2.4   Family circumstances identified in women entrepreneurs

Circumstances	Definition
Family: Role of the woman in the family	When entrepreneurial activity is closely linked to the woman's role of mother; the enterprise is seen as a way of fulfilling the role of mother through the generation of work positions for the children and the husband/partner, an independent source of income and security for members of the family.
Family: Voluntary family succession	The woman enters the entrepreneurial environment following a family line of succession: the father/mother/tutor gives her the possibility of working and directing the family enterprise and maintaining the continuity of the enterprise over time. Family succession is voluntary when the woman entrepreneur has the initiative because she wants to work in the family enterprise.
Family: Family succession by opportunity	When the family succession takes place because the relative invites the woman to be a part of the enterprise; entrepreneurship arises as a work opportunity in the family enterprise.
Family: Forced family succession	When the family succession occurs because some family circumstance forces the woman to join the family enterprise. Entrepreneurship happens as a result of the obligation to play a role within the family.
Family: Need for a flexible schedule	The circumstance refers to the woman's requirement of a work schedule that allows her to combine her responsibilities at work with those of the household and child care.

Table 2.5   Personal circumstances identified in women entrepreneurs

Circumstances	Definition
Personal: Presence of an entrepreneur role model	When the woman has an entrepreneurial role model who provides knowledge, motivation, support and/or courage.
Personal: Relatives who motivate and support entrepreneurship	When the woman entrepreneur has people close to her (parents/tutors/relatives/friends/acquaintances/partner/husband) that motivate her towards entrepreneurship. They may be parents who motivate the personal and professional development of their children through better educational levels and access to opportunities; role models who represent examples of work and achievement; partners who promote entrepreneurship, and so on.
Personal: Personal dissatisfaction	When the woman chooses entrepreneurship to "have something important to do", when her economic needs are covered and the enterprise is a source of personal satisfaction rather than necessary income.
Personal: Specific opportunity	When the woman chooses entrepreneurship for some specific opportunity, for example, the opportunity to acquire the enterprise she works in.

Table 2.6   Motives identified in women entrepreneurs

Motives	Definition
Motive of achievement	Related to carrying out a task that has a certain degree of difficulty and that needs to be developed swiftly and independently, in addition to surpassing obstacles and reaching a level of excellence (Murray, 1938, p. 164). This need to reach excellence motivates surpassing obstacles and striving to do difficult things as well and as fast as possible (Murray, 1938).
Motive of autonomy	Related to the desire to be independent and act according to her own will, without being subject to pressure or coercion exerted by an authority or by others in general (Murray, 1938).
Motive of achievement	Related to carrying out a task that has a certain degree of difficulty and that needs to be developed swiftly and independently, in addition to surpassing obstacles and reaching a level of excellence (Murray, 1938, p. 164). This need to reach excellence motivates surpassing obstacles and striving to do difficult things as well and as fast as possible (Murray, 1938).
Motive of autonomy	Related with the desire to be independent and act according to her own will, without being subject to pressure or coercion exerted by an authority or by others in general (Murray, 1938).
Motive of affiliation	Related to the need to establish links of cooperation and reciprocity, as well as the wish to gain the affections of a significant person (Murray, 1938).
Motive of power	Related to the need to control the feelings and behaviour of others; the wish to exert influence over others using suggestion, seduction, persuasion or commands, and; persuading others to act according to one's wishes or needs (Murray, 1938, p. 152).

There is rarely a sole circumstance or an only motive influencing a woman's decision to choose the entrepreneurial activity; entrepreneurship results from a combination of several circumstances or motives, that is, the factors cannot be considered as mutually exclusive and the same person can be influenced by many circumstances and many motives at the same time. Table 2.7 shows the matrix of circumstances and motives identified in each case. Results show a variety of patterns of factors that have motivated women to become entrepreneurs. Each case can be categorized into several circumstances and motives, which is why the number of total cases is higher than the number of informant women.

The patterns of personal circumstances show that two factors have an important influence on the stimulation of entrepreneurial activity: (a) the existence of people who motivate and support entrepreneurship; and (b) the presence of an entrepreneurial role model. These factors have not been clearly considered in previous literature. In the first case, they are people close to the women's life that motivate them towards entrepreneurship, help them in their personal and professional development, and give them access to opportunities and role models that represent examples of work and achievement.

Results show that this circumstance is found in most women entrepreneurs: the women declare having people close to them who motivated them towards entrepreneurship, a father figure or a partner who promoted the formation of the enterprise. This kind of support has a very important component of emotional support, that is, the presence of some relative, friend or acquaintance who motivated her and encouraged her to create the enterprise. In most cases, this role is assumed by the parents or husband/partner of the woman entrepreneur. The entrepreneurial role model, in turn, constitutes a source of knowledge on entrepreneurial activity and an example for the women to emulate or use as experience before creating their enterprises. The entrepreneur role model is the example of entrepreneurial activity for the woman, gives her courage to decide to become an entrepreneur and allows her to access the knowledge needed to develop the entrepreneurial activity.

With regards to the motives identified in the study, all informant women have expressed *achievement* and *autonomy*, while few of them have expressed *affiliation* and *power*. These results are not consistent with what was found in Singapore by Lee (1996), who pointed out that women were motivated by a high need of achievement and power, while the *autonomy* and *affiliation* motives were moderate.

Table 2.7   Analysis of cases of women entrepreneurs

Case	Economic	Work	Family	Personal	Motive of achievement	Motive of autonomy	Motive of affiliation	Motive of power
A			X	X	X			X
B		X		X	X	X		
C				X	X	X		
D	X			X	X		X	
E		X		X	X	X		
F		X		X	X	X		
G		X		X	X			
H	X	X		X	X	X		
I		X		X	X	X	X	
J				X	X		X	
K	X	X		X	X	X	X	
L				X	X	X		
M	X			X	X	X		X
N	X		X	X	X	X	X	
O	X			X	X	X		
P	X			X	X			
Q			X	X	X		X	
R	X			X	X	X	X	
S	X	X		X	X	X		
T	X			X		X		
U	X		X	X	X	X		X
V	X			X	X	X		
W			X	X	X	X		
X	X	X	X	X	X	X		
Total	13	9	6	24	23	18	7	3

Women expressed *achievement* as: (a) the need to "reach a dream" they have always had; (b) a high capacity of work and personal effort to keep the entrepreneurial project going; (c) the passion shown for their entrepreneurial activity; (d) the active search for success in their entrepreneurial activities; (e) oriented willingness to assume challenges and take opportunities; (f) a high level of commitment and perfection in their activities, that is, the intention to assume more responsibilities than those directly entrusted, in order to distinguish themselves from others and try to "do things best than the rest"; (g) a high motivation to learn, an expression of curiosity that puts them in a situation of continuous learning; and (h) an intention to achieve economic success, since entrepreneurship offers unlimited development opportunities.

Women expressed *autonomy* through: (a) a desire to be "their own boss"; (b) the need to achieve economic independence from their husbands/partners or family, which generates a self-worth that gives them pride and satisfaction; (c) the need to control their own lives; (d) the need to have something they can control and through which they can express themselves; and (e) the need to be autonomous in their decisions and not have to wait for other people to approve their decisions.

Women entrepreneurs expressed *affiliation* through their desire to obtain social value by earning the esteem of an important group, mainly their family. Women entrepreneurs expressed *power* through their desire for status and to direct other people's activities.

The literature shows a wide range of possible motivations for women. In Asia and Latin America, Kantis et al. (2002) found to be factors the need for achievement and personal development, and the desire to be their own bosses. The factors found in the United States are related to the need for achievement, the need for independence, the need of a greater work satisfaction, economic needs, frustration with work, unemployment, boredom or widowhood, opportunity, status, power and job security, the opportunity to undertake challenges, self-determination and the need to balance family and work responsibilities (Schwartz, 1976; Goffee and Scase, 1985; Brush, 1992; Hisrich and Brush, 1986; Buttner and Moore, 1997). In Canada, the factors identified include the fulfilment of an old dream, the desire to use their own talents, recognition from others, the logical continuation of work experience, the need to control their own lives, the need to stay up to date, the use of their own talents, economic need, the need for something of their own that they can control and through which they can express themselves, the creation of jobs for the family, and to have a better quality of life because the job is too demanding and limits motherhood (Lee-Gosselin and Grisé, 1990). In South Africa, the factors include the need for independence, for material incentives and for achievement, and the need to keep learning and to earn more money to survive (Mitchell, 2004).

Previous literature has frequently explained women entrepreneurs' motives for starting their enterprises through *push* and *pull* factors (Buttner and Moore, 1997) and the family environment (Orhan and Scott, 2001). The push factors are those that have pushed the woman to become an entrepreneur, such as insufficient family income, dissatisfaction in paid jobs, difficulty in finding work and the need for a flexible schedule.

The pull factors refer to self-fulfilment, independence from a hierarchical structure or the desire for increased status (Orhan and Scott, 2001). The push factors are related to the negative circumstances that lead to entrepreneurship and the pull factors, to internal positive motives or needs that drive entrepreneurial activity. However, the push/pull model does not clearly distinguish external circumstances from personal motives, and assumes that the push factors have a negative connotation.

The literature makes no clear distinction between women's motives and the circumstances under which they become entrepreneurs. The results are consistent with many of the motives found in the literature explaining the factors that influence entrepreneurship. According to the literature, the need for a flexible schedule to tend to family responsibilities is a very powerful motive of women to become entrepreneurs, as is the existence of a male-dominated work environment (Orhan and Scott, 2001; Minniti et al., 2005).

However, the results of the study (Avolio, 2010) show that the need for a flexible schedule and the existence of a male-dominated work environment are not motives that have stimulated women to become entrepreneurs. The results do not reinforce what the literature indicates, since in many cases women face more complicated schedules than those of dependent jobs. With regards to male-dominated work environment, the results show that women do not perceive this situation or that they evaluate it differently than described in the literature (Carter and Cannon, 1992). None of them declared feeling that a male-dominated work environment impeded them from reaching any professional position. On the contrary, they consider that the male-dominated is another challenge to prove their professional capabilities. When they had to face a male-dominated culture, women answer with the way they were able to overcome such barriers. This does not mean that the male-dominated culture has not allowed them to reach a better position in a dependent job, but rather, shows that these women do not perceive it that way.

The circumstances surrounding women's decisions to become entrepreneurs that were found are explained in detail below.

Economic Circumstances

BASIC ECONOMIC NEED

This circumstance includes those women who did not have another choice, and saw the need to start an enterprise to earn money. There is no doubt that there are incentives in any entrepreneurial initiative that permit the owner to satisfy economic needs. However, this circumstance refers to the situation in which the economic responsibility of the woman (sole or principal income earner in the household) is the main circumstance that motives her to create an enterprise when she has no other alternative to support her family. As opposed to the *dissatisfaction with the family income* motive, the enterprise is seen as the way to support the woman and her family. For example:

> *Why did you decide to start your enterprise? Because I had to defeat hunger and poverty. That was my mission and my task. And I have had to do it, and I've done it with effort. (Vilma 107:107)*

DISSATISFACTION WITH FAMILY INCOME

This circumstance is not necessarily associated with deprivation, but rather to the perception that current income is not sufficient to cover the needs of the woman and her family. Even if it is enough to cover the basic expenses of the household, the family income is not enough to generate savings, to develop economically, to offer better opportunities to her children, to have money for entertainment, and to have a better standard of living for the woman and her family. This dissatisfaction is a voluntary wish to have more than one has, and not a need for basic sustenance. It can be expressed as: "We can live, but we want more income to increase our standard of living." For example:

> *What happens is that you want certain things, certain comforts. And you can't. Or you want to improve something but can't. I mean, you have to limit yourself. That's it. That's what drove me to work more hours, to stay longer. I mean, I wanted to have better things. I didn't want to be with the same things. (Miriam 100:100)*

Here in Peru, if you don't make up your own source of work, what do you live with? You have to think "what can I do", if my husband goes to work and gets a minimum wage, and if I go out, the same. And while we go out to work, our children are abandoned, that's what I've never liked, for the parents to abandon their children. That's what I say: Peruvians have to be creative, create their own enterprises, even if it is, I don't know, painting stones, making hair scrunchies. (Francisca 103:103)

Work Circumstances

DIFFICULTIES IN FINDING A JOB

This circumstance refers to when a woman does not find a job because of lack of opportunities in the labour market for her skills, because of her age or for her lack of education. It can be expressed as: "I have always been an entrepreneur, I did not find work opportunities, and entrepreneurship was my only option." For example:

Because there was a moment I was looking for a job and I said: "now what do I do? I can't find a job." But in a moment I said "I have to start it and I have to do it myself." (Teresa 235:236)

When you're over 30 or 35, you don't get job offers anymore, even though, I have friends that would give me a job in a restaurant. (Margarita 24:25)

LACK OF PERSPECTIVES FOR PROFESSIONAL GROWTH

This circumstance refers to the woman who has few possibilities of a promotion in her dependent job; she perceives that getting promoted or having a better work position is too difficult. She believes she cannot continue improving her position, and this generates frustration. This can be stated as: "I have a job, but I can't improve my position." This lack of prospects for professional growth can be due to a lack of opportunities or due to non-explicit discrimination. Sometimes there is an invisible barrier that makes promotion from her job position impossible. It is not about not having enough income to cover their needs or desires but about not feeling the professional satisfaction and prospects for advancement in their dependent job. For example:

Because we faced the need to create an enterprise, because our career went upwards. Because it went upwards, it would reach a point when we wouldn't be able to achieve management positions ... or higher. Then we said "What else will there be in the future for us?" Being young and very young managers. Then we said "There must be something we can do, something of our own, something if this ends one day." A "stable" job, shall we say, because there are no stable jobs nowadays. What's left for us? Then we decided to start an enterprise. (Gabriela 229:229)

FRUSTRATION WITH WORK FOR ECONOMIC REASONS

This circumstance refers to a situation in which the job the woman has, or those she can get, do not pay her what she considers she deserves or what she thinks she needs to feel satisfied, and she considers herself to be inadequately paid. It can be stated as: "I have a job, but I don't like it because I earn too little." For example:

Because when I worked with him, I realized I was the strength of his salon, I realized people came in looking for me, for the motivation I had to do the job ... Then I looked at my income, because back then I took in 500 soles a week, although he only gave me 30 per cent, I did my calculations, and with what I produced I could pay the rent and people to help me. I paid attention to my income, and that encouraged me a lot to take off and make progress. (Enit 202:203)

DISSATISFIED WITH A MALE-DOMINATED WORK ENVIRONMENT

This happens when a dependent job does not offer a woman the same conditions and opportunities as it does to men, for example, when a woman perceives that she is being offered fewer opportunities for promotion or less pay for the same level of responsibility as men.

The results show that women do not perceive this situation or that they evaluate it in a different way than described in the literature (Carter and Cannon, 1992). None declared feeling that a male-dominated work environment had prevented them from reaching a work position. On the contrary, they feel that male dominance is another challenge to prove their work capability. When referring to situations where they had to face a male dominance, women answer by pointing out how they were able to overcome those barriers. This does not mean that male dominance has not prevented them from reaching a better job position, but shows that women do not perceive it that way. For example:

Do you feel you were discriminated against for being a woman in any of your former jobs? Well, I don't think so, because I've always been seen as a fighting woman, a strong woman. And they never discriminated against me. (Jesusa 220:222)

Do you think that a male attitude of thinking that "women can't" was a factor in your starting your enterprise? Yes, I am more encouraged to do better, to show them that I can. (Ruth 204:206)

LOGICAL CONTINUATION OF PROFESSIONAL GROWTH

This circumstance refers to women with a broad experience in a dependent job who consider entrepreneurship to be the logical continuation of their professional growth. It can be stated as: "I have worked all my life, now is the moment to have something of my own." Such is the case of Gabriela, who considered it was the time to start her own enterprise because she had had enough experience of being self-employed.

Family Circumstances

ROLE OF THE WOMAN IN THE FAMILY

This circumstance appears when the entrepreneurial activity is deeply connected to the role of mother and her function in the family. The results show that women seek: (a) to involve their children in their enterprises so they can learn their operation; (b) that their children have access to a better education than the women attained, so they can apply that knowledge to improve the management of the enterprise; (c) to generate their own source of work for their growing children; (d) so their children will have the capacity to develop themselves and face life's ups and downs; (e) to give economic security to their family, the kind of security they yearn for. For example:

How did you come to own the enterprise? Well, the first one was when my Dad was sick, as I told you before. The fear that something might happen to him and that all this would go bankrupt and we would end up with nothing. I am a person who has come a long way, and I know what it is like to be at the bottom. And that encouraged me too. I want more for my family … to have more in the future … things that I don't have. And the experience I am

getting, if God permits it, can someday open a larger enterprise. Leave this
enterprise to my siblings. That's what I wish for. (Silvia 190:190)

Which were your objectives and your vision when you started your enterprise?
When I saw that the business was growing, I opened two more pizza parlors.
I opened a third one. I gave two to one of my sons, and one to the other. They
left them to go to the United States and Rome. (Liliana 221:222)

FAMILY SUCCESSION

This circumstance refers to the situation in which women choose
entrepreneurship through family succession. In which the father/mother/tutor
gives her the possibility of working and managing the family enterprise. Family
succession can be voluntary, because of an opportunity or need.

Voluntary family succession is when the woman entrepreneur has the
initiative, because she wants to work in the family enterprise. The family
enterprise turns out to be the natural way of entering the working world. In
the cases when the woman becomes an entrepreneur as a product of family
succession, previous work experience is not necessarily related to the line of
business of the enterprise and the family background holds more weight.

Succession by opportunity happens when the relative offers the woman
the chance of becoming part of the enterprise, as is the case of Lorena Boston,
cited below. Family succession by need happens because of an obligation; some
family circumstance forces the woman to enter the family enterprise. When
the woman does not enter into the enterprise voluntarily, she is usually not
prepared for it. For example:

How did you come to run the enterprise? Because of family succession.
Because of the need itself. Because of the worry that something could
happen to dad. This way the enterprise would be in my hands and my
family would be protected. (Silvia 149:150)

Did you have any special reason to become an entrepreneur? Let's say
life took me there and I did it. That is, it's not something I thought about
too much, really. As I told you, since I was little it was: "Lorena will take
control of the enterprise", "Lorena has the qualities" ... so I didn't think
much about it, really. I got in somehow, and I really like it. I like what I
do. (Lorena 107:107)

Personal Circumstances

PRESENCE OF AN ENTREPRENEURIAL MODEL

This circumstance refers to an entrepreneur who plays the role model for the woman, a source of knowledge and a model for the women to emulate or use as prior experience for creating their own enterprises. The entrepreneurial model is the example of entrepreneurial activity for the woman, gives her courage in her decision to become an entrepreneur and allows her access to the knowledge needed to develop her enterprise. For example:

> *Dad was never interested in the business, but Mom was; she raised her four children in such a way that she sent us to different places to learn more about bakery, since there was no university were we lived. (Ruth 51:51)*

> *I worked one year with my teacher and another two with his brother. He had hair salons in Miraflores, Surquillo and Rímac. What did you learn there? I learnt a lot: to run a hair salon, to deal with clients, to have good sense, to manage some situations. (Enit 85:89)*

> *I have always admired people who start from scratch and succeed, as is the case of the Wong family and the Añaños family, from Kola Real. I have always liked to investigate, to read about these successful experiences of various entrepreneurs in the country, and there are a lot. (Gabriela 269:269)*

THE EXISTENCE OF PEOPLE WHO MOTIVATE AND SUPPORT ENTREPRENEURSHIP

This circumstance is found when the woman entrepreneur has people close to her personal life (parents/tutors/relatives/partner/husband) who encourage her towards entrepreneurship. They may be parents who encourage the personal and professional development of their children through better educational levels and access to opportunities, models who represent examples of work and achievement, partners who promote entrepreneurship, and so on.

The results show that this circumstance is found in most women entrepreneurs; the women declare having people close to them who encouraged them towards entrepreneurship. This type of support has a very important component of emotional support, that is, the presence of some relative, friend or acquaintance that motivated her and encouraged her to create the enterprise. In many cases, this role is assumed by the parents or husband/partner of the woman entrepreneur. For example:

> *My father has been my example of perseverance and struggle. He has been a big example for me … maybe I got the tenacity from him. I never heard him complaining or whining. Rather, one of his mottos, in response to being asked he feels, was to respond: "I'm struggling, because life is a constant struggle, and I will stop struggling the day I die." (Gloria 39:39)*

PERSONAL DISSATISFACTION

Women entrepreneurs can start an enterprise "to have something important to do" when their economic needs are covered and they are looking for a source of personal satisfaction rather than economic income. For example:

> *Why did you decide to establish your restaurant? No: I started the business because I had to do something. When I finished my job, I didn't work for a year, playing day and night. And I told myself: "This can't go on, let's do something." (Liliana 182:182)*

SPECIFIC OPPORTUNITY

A specific opportunity appears when a woman faces an opportunity to start an enterprise and decides to assume the challenge of entrepreneurial activity. If such specific circumstances had not happened, these women would probably not have chosen the entrepreneurial activity.

NEED FOR A FLEXIBLE SCHEDULE

The need for a schedule that allows women to combine their work and home responsibilities, and to have a better quality of life, since dependent jobs tend to be very demanding and limiting for a mother is another circumstance mentioned in the literature (Carter and Cannon 1992; Orhan and Scott, 2001). However, one study (Avolio, 2010) shows that this circumstance does not have an important effect on women who choose entrepreneurship. The need for a flexible schedule is associated with the desire to spend more time with the children or doing the housework. Nonetheless, women entrepreneurs, rather than having more time for family activities, face longer work days than those with dependent jobs.

Motives

Avolio (2010) shows that women entrepreneurs have expressed their motives to be: *achievement, autonomy, affiliation* and *power*.

MOTIVE OF ACHIEVEMENT

With regards to *achievement*, women entrepreneurs have stated that entrepreneurship is a source of personal satisfaction. The motive of *achievement* is expressed in women through: (a) a drive to "reach a dream"; (b) a high capacity to work to achieve their goals; (c) a passion they feel for their entrepreneurial activity; (d) a desire to seek success; (e) a desire for personal, professional and economic improvement; (f) a capacity to take on challenges; (g) a desire to "do things better than others"; (h) a high motivation to learn; and (i) amotivation to obtain economic success.

Drive to reach a dream

Some women express a motive of "reaching a dream" they have always had, regardless of their economic resources or educational level. One may consider that women with a low educational and economic level become entrepreneurs exclusively out of economic need. However, these cases show that the lack of education and economic resources is not decisive in entrepreneurship motivated by an economic need. In this group of persons, "reaching a dream" is mentioned more often than the economic issue. Facing a lack of economic resources, these women could have sought a dependent job, but they considered it absurd to look for a job if they had the capacity needed to start their own enterprise. For example:

> *Did you always want to be an entrepreneur? I always had this feeling that I could do something myself. A need for achievement? Maybe for a new challenge. (Gabriela 276:279)*

> *What made me … what happens is that I've always wanted to have my own thing since I was very young, something that is mine, it's as if you have something inside you that tells you "Well, you can't work for others, you have to have your own thing, work for yourself." They say that, at the beginning, it is like a staircase, like steps: at first you work for others, then you work for yourself, and then you give work to others. I think those are the stairs you climb on your way to success, as they say. Well, I*

never stopped to think I had to give employment to others, but now I am thankful for that. (Miriam 96:96)

Capacity for work and personal effort

The results show that women entrepreneurs have a high level of dedication to their work activities, find personal satisfaction in these activities, and have a high capacity to work. For example:

You always see me loaded with work. Of course I have defects, like every other human being. And I think one of my big defects is that I am a workaholic. (Gabriela 143:143)

Passionate about what they do

Women entrepreneurs are passionate for their enterprises, their job is not only a source of income; it is a source of satisfaction. For example:

Work for me is really a joy. And that's what I try to teach my children. That they have to do whatever they undertake with love and passion. Really, that passion to do all things you undertake in life. Do things with love and a lot of patience. (Gabriela 137:137)

Active search for success

Women entrepreneurs show an active desire to achieve success in their activities:

For example, I was a businesswoman since I was seven. How come? I sold everything because, as I told you, my parents were farmers. I sold bananas, oranges, cilantro ... there was everything for me to sell. Did you parents ask you to do it? No, they never forced me to, it's just that I saw so many things go bad, like the bananas, and I said "Why don't I sell them?" (Enit 42:48)

I wanted something of my own, my house, and a car because I didn't have one ... I got my apartment with Mi Banco. (Enit 240:241)

Of course, I was active and he wasn't. He was happy on a minimum wage. He complained, saying, "You like working too much; you should give us some space." (Ruth 88:88)

I started as a secretary, but my boss realized very soon that he could send me to the campsites of his supplying partner. He sent me to the World Bank. I fixed things up for him. That's how I ended up having my own secretary. I moved from help to management. (Liliana 231:231)

Desire for self-improvement

Women entrepreneurs display a desire for personal, professional and economic improvement, they are eager to learn everything they can and look to perfect themselves more and more. For example:

Why did you decide to create you enterprise? Yes, to be big. To be big and one day depend on what is mine. And I have really lived with some Arabs who were really, really rich. So I have really lived in a really luxurious house. I have eaten good food. I said: "Why can't I live like this too?" I can too. I was young. That's what led me to create my enterprise. (Jesusa 219:219)

Did you always want to be an entrepreneur? I always had this feeling that I could do something for myself ... Maybe a new challenge. (Gabriela 276:279)

Capacity of undertaking challenges

Women who show a desire to take up challenges and grab opportunities. For example:

This lady asked me, because she saw me everyday looking for a job, when she told me: "My friend needs a stylist, it's an A1 salon in San Juan de Lurigancho," "but it's a pity you're not a stylist," then I answered: "of course I am a stylist," because I was desperate, I showed her my certificate from a basic course I took for a year, and then she decided to recommend me for the job, and gave me a letter to go to San Juan de Lurigancho. (Enit 61:61)

No. It's just that the owner … In this salon … three owners came and went. I stayed with every owner that opened the hair salon. I stayed … Suddenly he said: "I'm going to close the place." I said "Ah, well then." I was going to go back to work in an accountant's office with a friend. And one of the clients told me: "Monica, you know how this works, why don't you take the chance?" And that's how it began. I started with two armchairs, two mirrors. There were days I didn't work at all. (Monica 44:44)

Do things better than the rest

Women entrepreneurs show a desire to perfect themselves, a high level of commitment and perfection in their activities, the wish to assume more responsibilities than those directly entrusted, which distinguishes them from the rest of people. For example:

Because when I worked with this gentleman, I realized I was the strength of his salon, I realized the people came looking for me … People even mistook me for the owner in each salon I worked in, because of the will, the devotion I had for each job, because I was always checking and helping. (Enit 202:202)

High motivation to learn

Women entrepreneurs show a great motivation to learn new things, a curiosity that allows them to continue learning. For example:

Did you have any experience in your youth that contributed to your decision of starting your own enterprise? Yes, I worked in the house of very important people. People with a lot of money, who treat you bad sometimes because you're the housekeeper. And well, that's what encouraged me to learn someday and be someone. Maybe I couldn't study because I didn't have the chance. My mother was very young, I was very young, I was eight years old. But I wanted to learn something. To get ahead. (Jesusa 246:247)

Then I decided to start this business because of these reasons. One, because I had already worked in everything. I liked working. And I always wanted to work like this, with children. That was when I travelled to see how it works. I went to the United States. I was in Buenos Aires with someone who does this kind of things. (Teresa 195:196)

Achieving economic success

This circumstance refers to the fact that sometimes a dependent job does not allow women to achieve economic success, while the possibilities for economic success in entrepreneurial activities are unlimited. Some women become entrepreneurs "to be rich," since "you will never become a millionaire" in a dependent job. For example:

> *When I was with the father of my children, I said: "When I have my own business I will buy my own clothes, my own shoes," the things I need, right? Or buy things I needed at home. I am doing all that, little by little. Though there's still a lot to do, right? A long way to go. (Carmela 543:543)*

MOTIVE OF AUTONOMY

Autonomy is expressed in women through: (a) the need to "be you own boss" and the fact that "I don't like anyone giving me orders"; (b) autonomy from her partner or family; (c) the need to control their own lives; (d) having something they can control and through which they can express themselves; and (e) autonomy in decision making. For example:

> *My mother always told me: "My girl, you were not born to receive orders; you have been born to give them." I always remember she said that … I felt really good then, my Mom is right, I always had that in mind, when sometimes the owner made me work too much, from 15 to 16 hours a day, it was too much, and I only felt better with what Mom said, and I always kept it in my mind, and I always say it to my children too. (Ruth 153:155)*

> *I didn't need anybody else to order me around, because our parents weren't ordered around either. Be ourselves, have our own things, be proud of what we had. (Rosa 112:112)*

Autonomy is also expressed when entrepreneurial activity permits women to achieve economic independence from their husbands/partners or family; when women change from being a passive objective of the couple and from being economically dependent on their partners or relatives to achieving their own value, which fills them with pride and satisfaction. The motive that encourages entrepreneurship is economic, but not out of economic need, but autonomy. For example:

I had to pay for it all myself, no one helped me. And your parents? I told my parents not to send me anything because I was working. I needed things, but I liked to do things by myself. (Ruth 41:45)

Why did you decide to start your own enterprise? To have my own time. My own money. It was nice. (Jesusa 260:262)

More than anything, to be independent. I was already tired of working as a slave for others, because when Christmas or Independence Day came, they gave me a 10 soles bonus. (Carmela 842:842)

Other women expressed their autonomy through the need to have something of their own, something they could control and through which they could express themselves, for example:

Then we used to say "What else will there be in the future for us?" Being young, and very young managers. Then we said "There must be something we can do" Something of our own. Something if this ends one day ... (Gabriela 229:229)

I always liked the business. I always wanted to generate something on my own, but I didn't know what. And then the salon opportunity presented itself. (Monica 270:270)

What motivated to start your enterprise? Two things: One, I always wanted to have something of my own. And two, in the market, there wasn't what I wanted to do. (Teresa 193:196)

Autonomy in entrepreneurial women is also evident in their independence to make decisions. These women do not wait for their parents, husbands or other authority figures to approve their plans or decisions. For example:

I make the decisions, I tell Paco, "Paco, I am doing this." (Ruth 205:205)

The satisfaction of feeling that something is yours ... of course, it is yours, and if you want to earn a little more, you sacrifice a little more, or if you want to increase your capital, your sales, you do more, or put some, for example, if I want to put some dishes on the menu, I put them and do it. (Carmela 845:846)

MOTIVE OF POWER

Women expressed power through their desire for status, having an active leadership role in groups, organizing and directing the activities of other people. The entrepreneurial activity for these women is a way of showing their own value to themselves and to others. For example:

> My Mom always comes here. When she knew I was working in a bakery, she was very happy, and she always told me: "My girl, you were not born to receive orders, but to give them." I always remember that she used to say that. (Ruth 53:53)

> I always wanted a little power. And now I have it. And that also fills me with pride and satisfaction. (Silvia 241:242)

MOTIVE OF AFFILIATION

This motive is expressed through entrepreneurial activity and is a social value, since it acts as a framework for a large part of the interactions established throughout life. For example:

> I think that, as I told you, showing what I am capable of doing. What made me do it? I mean, if my parents were both successful, if my relatives were successful, why couldn't I? I didn't want to be the ugly duckling in the family. If I had my parents, who could do everything they did, who could have all the money they had and could cover all the ground they did, why couldn't I? What do the other entrepreneurs have that I don't? (Doris 104:104)

References

Atlasti Qualitative Data Análisis Software (2007). 5.2.15 Released.

Avolio, B. (2010). *A Profile of Women Entrepreneurship in Peru: An Exploratory Study*. Doctoral Thesis.

Bennett, R. and Dann, S. (2000). The changing experience of Australian female entrepreneurs. *Australian Female Entrepreneurs, 7*(2), 75–83.

Blondet, C. and Montero, C. (1994). *La Situación de la Mujer en el Perú: 1980–1994 [The Situation of Women in Peru 1980–1994]*. Lima, Perú: Instituto de Estudios Peruanos.

Brush, C. (1992). Research on women business owners: Past trends, a new perspective and future directions. *Entrepreneurship Theory and Practice, 16*(4), 5–30.

Buttner, E. and Moore, D. (1997). Women's organizational exodus to entrepreneurship: Self-reported motivations. *Journal of Small Business Management, 35*(1), 34–46.

Carter, S. and Cannon, T. (1992). *Women as Entrepreneurs*. London: Academic Press.

Cooper, A. (1981). Strategic management: New ventures and small business. *Long Range Planning, 14*(5), 39–45.

Creswell, J. (2003). *Research Design: Qualitative, Quantitative and Mixed Methods Approaches*. Thousand Oaks, CA: Sage Publications.

Echeverri-Carroll, E. and Brandazza, D. (2002, abril). Empresarias decididas, Women entrepreneurs in the Americas. *Texas Business Review*. Retrieved 15 December 2003 from http://www.stexas.edu/depts/bbr/tbr.

Eisenhardt, K. (1989). Building theories from case study research. *Academy of Management Review, 14*(4), 532–550.

Feng, Y. (2005). *Study of Societal Cultural Impact on HRM Practices in Business Organizations: The Case of China*. Maastricht, The Netherlands: Maastricht School of Management.

Fernández-Abascal, E. (2001). *Manual de Motivación y Emoción [Manual of Motivation and Emotion]*. Madrid, España: Ed. Centro de Estudios Ramón Areces.

Glaser, B. and Strauss, A. (1967). *The Discovery of Grounded Theory*. Chicago: Aldine Publising Company.

Goffee, R. and Scase, R. (1985). *Women in Charge: The Experiences of Female Entrepreneurs*. London: George Allen and Unwin.

Hisrich, R. and Ayse Öztürk, S. (1999). Women entrepreneurs in a developing economy. *Journal of Management Development, 38*(2), 114–124.

Hisrich, R. and Brush, C. (1986). *The Woman Entrepreneur: Starting, Financing and Managing a Successful New Business*. Toronto, Canada: Lexington Books, D.C. Heath and Company.

Hisrich, R. and Brush, C. (1991). Antecedent influence on women-owned business. *Journal of Management Psychology, 2*(2), 9–16.

Hisrich, R. and Fan, Z. (1991). Women entrepreneurs in the People's Republic of China, an exploratory study. *Journal of Managerial Psychology, 6*(3), 3–12.

Hisrich, R. and Fulop, G. (1994). The role of women entrepreneurs in Hungary's transition economy. *International Studies of Management and Organization, 24*(4), 100–118.

Hisrich, R. and O'Brien, M. (1981). The woman entrepreneur from a business and sociological perspective. In Vesper, K.H. (Ed.), *Frontiers on Entrepreneurship Research* (pp. 21–39). Wellesley, MA: Babson College Center for Entrepreneurship.

Hisrich, R. and O'Brien, M. (1982). The woman entrepreneur as a reflection of the type of business. In Vesper, K.H. (Ed.), *Frontiers of Entrepreneurship Research* (pp. 54–67). Wellesley, MA: Babson College Center for Entrepreneurship.

Inman, K. (2000). *Women´s Resources in Business Start-up, A Study of Black and White Women Entrepreneurs*. New York: Garland Publishing.

Instituto Nacional de Estadística e Informática. (2005a). *Perú: Compendio Estadístico 2005*. Lima, Perú: Instituto Nacional de Estadística e Informática.

Instituto Nacional de Estadística e Informática. (2005b). *Perú: Encuesta Demográfica y de Salud Familiar*. Lima, Perú: Instituto Nacional de Estadística e Informática.

Instituto Nacional de Estadística e Informática. (2006a). *Condiciones de Vida en el Perú: Evolución 1997–2004*. Lima, Perú: Talleres de la Oficina Técnica de Administración del Instituto Nacional de Estadística e Informática.

Instituto Nacional de Estadística e Informática. (2006b). *Censo 2005: X de Población – V de Vivienda*. [Data File]. Lima, Perú: Instituto Nacional de Estadística e Informática.

Kantis, H., Ishida, M. and Komori, M. (2002). *Empresarialidad en Economías Emergentes: Creación y Desarrollo de Nuevas Empresas en América Latina y el Este del Asia*. Nueva York: Banco Interamericano de Desarrollo.

Lang, J. and Fries, S. (2006). A revised 10-item version of the achievement motives scale psychometric properties in German-speaking samples. *European Journal of Psychological Assessment, 22*(3), 216–224.

Lee, J. (1996). The motivation of women entrepreneurs in Singapore. *Women in Management Review, 11*(2), 18–29.

Lee-Gosselin, H. and Grisé, J. (April/May 1990). Are women owner-managers challenging our definitions of entrepreneurship? An in-depth survey. *Journal of Business Ethics, 9*(4), 423–433.

Marshall, C. and Rossman, G. (1999). *Designing Qualitative Research*. Thousand Oaks, CA: Sage Publications.

Maxwell, J. (1996). *Qualitative Research Design: An Integrative Approach*. Thousand Oaks, CA: Sage Publications.

McClelland, D. (1974). Sources of need for achievement. In McCLelland, D. and Steele, R. (Eds), *Human Motivation: A Book of Readings* (pp. 319–377). New Jersey: General Learning Press.

Miles, M. and Huberman, M. (1994). *Qualitative Data Analysis: An Expanded Sourcebook*. Thousand Oaks, CA: Sage Publications.

Minniti, M., Arenius, P. and Langowitz, N. (2005). *Global entrepreneurship monitor: 2004 report on women and entrepreneurship*. Retrieved on 10 January 2006 from http://www.gemconsortium.org//download.asp?id=478.

Mitchell, B. (2004). Motives of entrepreneurs: A case study of South Africa. *The Journal of Entrepreneurship, 13*(2), 167–193.

Murray, H.A. (1938). *Explorations in Personality*. New York: Oxford University Press.

Neider, L. (1987). A preliminary investigation of female entrepreneurs in Florida. *Journal of Small Business Management, 25*(3), 22–28.

Orhan, M. and Scott, D. (2001). Why women enter into entrepreneurship: An exploratory model. *Journal of Management Review, 16*(5/6), 232–242.

Real Academia Española (2001). *Diccionario de la lengua española [Dictionary of the Spanish Language] (22nd edn)*. Retrieved on 2 January 2008 from http://www.rae.es.

Reeve, J. (1994). *Motivación y Emoción [Motivation and Emotion]*. Barcelona, España: McGraw-Hill.

Rubin, H. and Rubin, I. (1995). *Qualitative Interviewing: The Art of Hearing Data*. Thousand Oaks, CA: Sage Publications.

Schwartz, E. (1976). Entrepreneurship: A new female frontier. *Journal of Contemporary Business, 5*(1), 47–76.

Serida, J., Borda, A., Nakamatsu, K., Morales, O. and Yamakama, P. (2005). *Global entrepreneurship monitor: Peru 2004–2005*. Lima, Perú: Ediciones ESAN.

Steers, R. and Braunstein, D. (1976). A behaviorally-based measure of manifest needs in work settings. *Journal of Vocational Behavior, 9*(2), 251–266.

Strauss, A. and Corbin, J. (1998). *Basics of Qualitative Research: Techniques and Procedures for Developing Grounded Theory*. Thousand Oaks, CA: Sage Publications.

Voeten, J. (2002). *Criteria to define women entrepreneurs who own and manage micro and small enterprises: Working paper 1 in the framework of the project "Training for women in micro and small enterprises, phase 2 (TWMSE2)"*. Maastricht, The Netherlands: Maastricht School of Management.

Yin, R. (2003). *Case Study Research: Concepts and Methods*. Thousand Oaks, CA: Sage Publications.

Zapalska, A. (1997). A profile of woman entrepreneurs and enterprises in Poland. *Journal of Small Business Management, 35*(4), 76–82.

3

Typology of Female Entrepreneurs

Emerging Conceptual Framework: Why do Women Become Entrepreneurs?

Avolio (2010) and previous literature have permitted the following conceptual framework to explain the various factors that have stimulated women to choose entrepreneurial activity, taking into consideration their background, the factors that motivated them to become entrepreneurs and the phase of their life cycle when they made this decision (Figure 3.1). The conceptual framework considers two dimensions: (a) the phase of their personal and work cycles when women choose entrepreneurship; and (b) the circumstances and motives that have stimulated women to become entrepreneurs. The circumstances and motives that have influenced the women's decision to choose entrepreneurship are not mutually excluding, that is, a same person may be influenced by several circumstances and motives simultaneously.

Various studies in developed countries have explored the possible motivations of women entrepreneurs, but have not integrated them into a conceptual framework that comprehensively explains why women become entrepreneurs, bearing in mind their background and the factors that stimulated them to choose entrepreneurial activity. Besides, the investigations that analyse the motivations of women entrepreneurs do not clearly differentiate the circumstances from the motives for choosing entrepreneurship, but present lists of isolated factors.

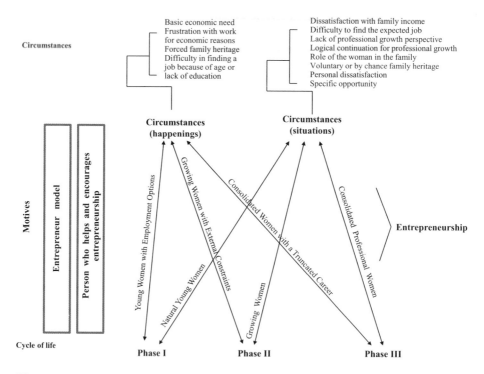

Figure 3.1   Emerging conceptual framework: Why do women become entrepreneurs?

The Life Cycle of Women Entrepreneurs

Avolio (2010) shows that women entrepreneurs' backgrounds are varied in terms demography, education, family and work, and cannot be considered as a single category. The study shows that women entrepreneurs differ from one another in their demographic characteristics and in their educational, work and family backgrounds.

These results are not consistent with Hisrich and Brush (1984), who found that women entrepreneurs in the United States have similar family background, education work experience, entrepreneurial characteristics, management skills and motivation; and that most women entrepreneurs are the first born of middle-class families in which the father was self-employed; half of them are married to men employed in professional or technical activities, and have two adolescent children on average; almost 70 per cent have basic education and many have university titles; their parents and husbands also have a good educational level; most of them do not have management knowledge, they have limited work experience, and when they do have it, it is in the area of services as teachers, management employees of middle level or secretaries.

It is not correct to establish a profile of women entrepreneurs that considers a single dimension, because it would be an inadequate simplification of their backgrounds. The profile of women entrepreneurs must consider the stage in their work and personal life cycles when they choose entrepreneurship. Carter and Cannon (1992) point out that the way that women face the start of their entrepreneurial activity is controlled by the stage in their life cycle in which this happens, that is, their age and domestic relationships. They indicate that the differentiation by life cycle is important because women start their enterprises at different moments in their lives and this affects the type of enterprise and their particular approach to ownership. Besides, Carter and Cannon (1992) point out that the previous work experience generates diverse motivations and aspirations with respect to enterprise ownership.

Avolio (2010) shows that women entrepreneurs can be grouped by their common experiences during the stages of their life cycle when they choose entrepreneurship. In order to categorize women into the phases of their life cycles, the following characteristics related to their background have been considered: (a) stage of life when they choose entrepreneurship; and (b) stage of professional/work experience measured in the number of years of work experience prior to entrepreneurship. The age when they choose entrepreneurship has not been determinant for the life cycle categorization, since it depends rather on the experiences of each person.

The life cycle phases when women choose entrepreneurship that have arisen in the study (Avolio, 2010) are:

PHASE I: YOUNG WOMEN

This phase is essentially defined by the lack of dependents and relatively scarce or lack of relevant work experience. This group includes women who decide to become entrepreneurs in the first phase of their family life cycle, when they have no children, may or may not have a husband/partner and have little work experience. Entrepreneurship for these women may be the product of a natural option (such as voluntary family succession or entrepreneurial spirit) or be due to the absence of other work alternatives.

PHASE II: GROWING WOMEN

This phase is essentially defined by the existence of dependents and an intermediate level of work experience. This considers women who choose entrepreneurship in the middle phase of their life cycle: They usually, but not always, have economically and emotionally dependent small children; some are married or have life partners, others are separated, or divorced or may have a partner; they have regular work experience. These women have chosen entrepreneurship after having abandoned their dependent jobs or other independent activities.

PHASE III: CONSOLIDATED WOMEN

This phase is essentially defined by women who have advanced work experience and are with or without dependents. This includes women who have dependent young children or economically dependent children, even though some may have no children. In any case, they have work experience of over 20 years and decide to become entrepreneurs in the last stage of their work cycle, as the goal of their work development or the logical continuation of their professional development. These women choose entrepreneurship as a result of a lack of work opportunities, or they are women who, eager to develop their own independent entrepreneurial activity, accumulate work experience as dependent employees and then leave a paid job to establish an enterprise as the goal of their professional path.

Typology of Women Entrepreneurs

Results show the variety of patterns the women followed, depending on the life cycle and the factors that stimulated them to become entrepreneurs. The conceptual framework makes it possible to understand the different profiles of women entrepreneurs, taking into consideration their backgrounds and factors that motivated them to become entrepreneurs.

The conceptual framework distinguishes between the circumstances, referred to as happenings, and situations. A *happening* is "something that happens, especially when it has some importance" and in the present study, it refers to objective circumstances that affect a woman's decision to become an entrepreneur, such as the death of the father in a family business, or the loss of a dependent job. A *situation* is defined as a "disposition of something with respect of the place it holds" and refers to the factors that influence a woman's decision to become an entrepreneur and that depend on the woman's own perception, such as her dissatisfaction with the family income or her lack of prospects for professional growth.

The circumstances referred to as happenings are basic economic need, family succession due to need, difficulty in finding a job and frustration with work because of economic reasons. The circumstances referred to as *situations* include dissatisfaction with the family income, opportunistic or voluntary family succession, the role of the woman in the family, the lack of prospects for professional growth or continued professional development, personal dissatisfaction or specific opportunity. The motives are present in all cases of women entrepreneurs, so they have not been used as criteria to differentiate the profiles.

The emerging conceptual framework reinforces the results in that women cannot be considered as a homogeneous group with a single set of characteristics and that the profile of women entrepreneurs must be expressed through a typology that represents their different experiences. The analysis identified six profiles of women entrepreneurs that express the different paths through which women achieve entrepreneurship, developed with the information presented in Table 3.1.

The profiles that resulted from the study are:

YOUNG WOMEN WITH EMPLOYMENT OPTIONS

This group comprises those women that have chosen entrepreneurial activity in the face of circumstances that gave them no choice other than entrepreneurship, and whose work choice resulted in an entrepreneurial activity. These are women who are in the first phase of their personal and work life cycle; they have no children or dependents, and have little work experience. The educational level of this group of women is usually only basic education, which limits their work options. These women chose entrepreneurship without any previous preparation, which is why they develop their own experience in the enterprise itself and are less prepared for entrepreneurial activity than women with other profiles. For example:

> I became an entrepreneur ... by a circumstance, rather than an experience. Considering that my dad was alone in the enterprise.

Table 3.1　　　Matrix of results from analysed cases

Case	Phase of the family and work life cycle	CE: basic economic need	CE: dissatisfaction with family income	CL: Frustration with work for economic reasons	CL: Difficulty to find a job	CL: Lack of prospects for professional growth	CL: Logical continuation of professional growth	CF: Forced family succession	CF: Voluntary family succession	CF: Role of the woman	CP: Relatives motivate and support entrepreneurship	CP: Entrepreneurial role model	CP: Personal Dissatisfaction	CP: Specific opportunity	Motive of achievement	Motive of autonomy	Motive of affiliation	Motive of power
A	I							X			X	X			X			X
B	I	X									X	X				X		
C	I										X	X			X	X		
D	I			X							X	X	X		X	X		
E	I	X										X		X	X		X	
F	II		X								X	X			X	X		
G	II		X							X	X	X			X	X		
H	II					X					X				X			
I	II		X			X	X				X	X			X	X		
J	II					X					X	X			X	X	X	
K	II											X		X	X		X	
L	II		X			X					X	X			X	X	X	
M	II										X	X		X	X	X		
N	II			X							X	X			X	X		X
O	II	X									X	X			X	X		
P	II	X								X	X	X			X	X	X	
Q	II	X									X	X			X			
R	II								X		X	X			X		X	
S	III				X					X	X	X			X	X		X
T	III	X									X	X			X	X		
U	III	X									X	X			X	X	X	
V	II	X			X					X	X	X			X	X		
W	III									X	X		X		X	X		
X	III		X	X							X	X			X	X		
Total		8	5	3	2	4	1	1	1	5	22	22	2	3	23	18	7	3

The moment came when he got sick and I was scared ... if something happens to Dad, this will go bankrupt ... The fear that something could happen to him and that everything could go bankrupt and we'd end up with nothing. (Silvia 150:150)

Why did you open your enterprise? Need. Poverty and hunger were killing me at six, seven and eight years old ... I had to defeat hunger and poverty. That was my mission and my task. And I had to do it, and I did it with effort. (Vilma 107:107)

The last job I had was that of a street vendor. I sold cakes, chicha morada, jello ... My husband helped ... I sold chicha in the mornings and pudding and jello in the afternoons. Then we started the bakery, in partnership with his cousin ... we got a place in Comas. We've been there for 18 years. (Marcelina 33:33)

GROWING WOMEN WITH EXTERNAL CONSTRAINTS

This group comprises those women who have chosen the entrepreneurial activity in the face of circumstances that gave them no other work alternative, because of some sort of external limitation. These women have chosen entrepreneurship in the second phase of their work and personal life cycle, after having some work experience.

They usually have economically dependent small or older children, and may or may not have a husband/partner. The educational levels of this group of women are varied, but they usually have technical or higher education. These are women who have worked dependently and have acquired some work experience. They have chosen entrepreneurship mainly because of economic reasons: to cover their basic needs or because of frustration at getting insufficient pay in their dependent job. For example:

Here in Peru, if you do not make up your own source of work, what do you live with? You have to think "what can I do", if my husband goes to work and gets paid a minimum wage, and if I go out, the same thing happens. And while we go out to work, our children are abandoned, that's what I've never liked, for the parents to abandon their children. That's what I say: Peruvians have to be creative, create his own enterprises, even if it is, I don't know, painting stones, making hair scrunchies. (Francisca 103:103)

Look, I had a debt of about 400,000 soles to pay, I had only saved 60,000 soles and I had to pay in six months, in about six months, which was the time they had given me to pay off all that debt ... and the shop caught fire. I've had to refinance, go to enterprises to ask them to help me, or some approached me themselves and gave me credit for a year ... I put a lot of effort to go on forward. Because of that I took over the shop. (Edna 120:120)

CONSOLIDATED WOMEN WITH A TRUNCATED CAREER

This group comprises those women who have chosen the entrepreneurial activity when faced with circumstances that gave them no other work alternative, and whose dependent activity has been cut short. These women have chosen entrepreneurship in the third phase of their personal and work life cycle, after accumulating considerable work experience. They may or not have children, and if they do, these are already young adults. These women have chosen entrepreneurship because of obligations, as an answer to their frustration for economic reasons. They may have not become entrepreneurs if they had been satisfied with their dependent jobs. For them, entrepreneurship offers the option of covering their basic economic needs. Although these women had no preparation before entrepreneurship, they have professional maturity, and reach entrepreneurship with a vast work experience. For example:

Yes, I worked in the house of very important people. With people with a lot of money who sometimes treat you bad because you're the housekeeper. And well, that was what motivated me to someday learn and be someone. Maybe I couldn't study because I didn't have the chance. My mother was very young, I was little, I was eight years old. But I wanted to learn something. To get ahead. (Jesusa 246:247)

Why did you decide to start you own enterprise? Above all to be independent. I had already gotten tired of working as a slave for others, because when Christmas or Independence Day came, they gave me a 10 soles bonus. (Carmela 842:842)

Why did you decide to start your own enterprise? What happened is that I ended up alone, I was a widow. I studied because of that, thinking about the future, of my daughters ... It was another way out for me ... you have to think, think about the future. You want to be stable. You can't go from one job to another forever. Besides, age is also an issue. More than anything, to have something on your own. Not working for someone else forever. You realize you can do it by yourself. (Rosaluz 104:104)

NATURAL YOUNG WOMEN

This group is formed of those women who have chosen entrepreneurial activity as a naturally desirable work alternative. These women can be considered to be "natives" of entrepreneurship. They are entrepreneurs from the first phase of their personal and work cycle; they have no children or dependents and have little to no work experience. Their educational level might be basic or superior; what is relevant is their natural preference towards the entrepreneurial activity. These women have chosen entrepreneurship as the natural way of practising their work activity, for example:

> *What made you decide to start your enterprise? Two things: One, I always wanted to have something of my own. And two, in the market, there wasn't what I wanted to do. So I had to create this job because I didn't see myself doing anything else. (Teresa 193:196)*

> *Why did we start our business? I think that was born in us. To be independent, not to depend on others. We saw that our parents worked independently. It wasn't anything new for us, it wasn't a thing from outer space, it was the natural thing to do, having a business. (Rosa 104:104)*

GROWING WOMEN

This group is formed by those women who have chosen the entrepreneurial activity as a personal development option after having developed work experience as dependent workers. These women have "migrated" from dependent activity to entrepreneurship as an alternative for professional development. They have taken the choice of entrepreneurship in the second phase of their personal and work life cycle, after having some work experience. They usually have economically and emotionally dependent small or older children, and may or may not have a partner.

They are women who have worked dependently and have accumulated some work experience, and have chosen entrepreneurship because of situations such as a voluntary family succession; a lack of prospects for professional growth in dependent jobs; consideration of entrepreneurship as the logical continuation of their professional development; or because they are dissatisfied with the family income that, even though enough to cover their basic needs, does not allow them to satisfy their expectations for a better quality of life. These women have not experienced external events that prevented them from choosing another work alternative, but the situations they perceive depend on their own perspective. The educational level of these women is varied, but all of them have entered the entrepreneurial activity after having gained the needed knowledge through their work experience. For example:

> *What made me create my enterprise ... what happens is that, ever since I was little, I've wanted to have something of my own, it's like you have something inside you that says: "Well, you can't work for others, you have to have your own thing, work for yourself." (Miriam 96:96)*

> *Why did you decide to create your own enterprise? No. It's just that the owner ... In this salon ... three owners came and went. I stayed with every owner that opened the hair salon. I stayed ... Suddenly he said: "I'm going to close the place." I said "Ah, well then." I was going back to work in an accountant's office with a friend. And one of the clients told me: "Monica, you know how this works, why don't you take the chance?" And that's how I began. (Monica 44:44)*

> *Why did you decide to create your own enterprise? I wanted something of my own. Do my own thing. I didn't have any more there, that is, nowhere to grow. Because over me there was my boss, the owner of the enterprise, I couldn't be her owner, and I don't know, I decided to start my own enterprise. (Liliana Minera)*

> *Why did you decide to create your own enterprise? Because we faced the need to create an enterprise, because our career went upwards. Because it went upwards, it would reach a point when we wouldn't be able to achieve any management positions ... or higher ... Then we said "There must be something we can do." Something of our own. Something if this ends one day. A "stable" job, shall we say, because there are no stable jobs nowadays. What's left for us? Then we decided to start an enterprise. (Gabriela 220:229)*

> *Why did you decide to create your own enterprise? Let's say that life got me there and I assumed that role. I mean, it's not something I thought too much about, really. As I told you, since I was little it was: "Lorena will take the control of the enterprise," "Lorena has qualities" ... so I*

didn't think much about it, really. I got in somehow, and I really like it. I like what I do. (Lorena 107:107)

Why did you decide to create your own enterprise? Money. Basically money … you could be an excellent worker and you could be just a genius, do a lot of positive things, and you didn't earn more for that. The other thing was that, at that moment and for many more years, couldn't get promoted. (Cecilia 39:39)

CONSOLIDATED PROFESSIONAL WOMEN

This group is formed of those women who have chosen the entrepreneurial activity as the culmination of their work development, and after having gathered important work experience as dependent workers. These women have "migrated" from dependent activities to entrepreneurship as the culmination of their work career. They have chosen entrepreneurship in the third phase of their personal and work life cycle. They may or may not have children, and if they do, they are young adults.

They are women who have always worked for others and now want to work for themselves. They are women who have chosen entrepreneurship because of situations such as dissatisfaction with their current income or with their work as dependent workers; their decision is also related to the possibility of fulfilling their role in the family and generating work opportunities for their children and relatives. These women have not experienced external circumstances that have prevented them from choosing another work alternative; rather, the situations they perceive depend on their own perspective. The educational profile of these women is varied, but they have all entered the entrepreneurial activity after having acquired the required knowledge through their work experience, which is why they face entrepreneurship more prepared in work and personal terms than women entrepreneurs from other profiles. For example:

My Mom was very happy when she knew I was working in a bakery. She always told me: "My daughter, you haven't been born to receive orders, you were born to give them." I always remember she said that … I always bear it in mind, and I always repeat it to my children too. (Ruth 153:155)

How did you become the owner of a restaurant? When I was done with the enterprise. I said, Liliana, what do you like to do? I grabbed a piece of paper, and the first thing I wrote was, a building company, but I didn't have the money; second thing, sewing, because I like to sew, but I hadn't sewn a button in 14 years; cooking, I like cooking, cooking: OK. Cook what? I grabbed another piece of paper, chose the kind of restaurant that wouldn't tie me so much with too many different inputs. I choose a pizza parlour. The next day I was looking for a place. The first restaurant was born. (Liliana 28:28)

Conclusions

1. The driving factors for women to become entrepreneurs are a complex system of circumstances and motives. In no case does there seem to be a sole circumstance or sole motive impelling women to become entrepreneurs.

2. The factors that stimulated women to become entrepreneurs can be classified into: (a) motives; and (b) economic, work, family and personal circumstances. In other words, events or situations that appear in a certain context drove women to become entrepreneurs. The motives have an origin that is intrinsic to women, while circumstances are extrinsic to women and may impact entrepreneurship in a positive or negative way. These circumstances may be an objective event (such as the death of the father in a family enterprise or the loss of a dependent employment) or situations impacting entrepreneurship according to women's perceptions (such as dissatisfaction with the family income or a lack of professional growth prospects).

3. The economic circumstances that affect the decision to become an entrepreneur are economic need or dissatisfaction with family income. Work circumstances are difficulty to find employment due to lack of opportunities in the labour market because of a lack of skills or education, old age, lack of professional growth prospects, job frustration for economic reasons, or a belief that entrepreneurship is the logical continuation of professional growth. Family circumstances are when entrepreneurship is the means to comply with their family role or from a voluntary family succession, opportunities or necessity. Personal circumstances are an entrepreneurial model used as reference for women, relatives that promote and support entrepreneurship, personal dissatisfaction, or a specific opportunity.

4.   There are two factors that seem to have an important influence in women entrepreneurs' decision to become entrepreneurs and that have not been previously considered in the literature: (a) the existence of close people fostering, promoting and supporting in their entrepreneurship, or a paternal model or partner who promotes the creation of an enterprise; and (b) the existence of an entrepreneurial model that acts as a role model for women. In the first case, these are people who are close to women's lives who encourage them towards entrepreneurship, help them in their professional and personal development, give them access to opportunities and provide them with models that are examples of work and achievement. This kind of support has an important component of emotional backing, that is, the presence of a relative, a friend or someone they know who fosters and encourages her to create the enterprise. In many cases, this role is played by the parents or husband/partner of the women entrepreneur. The entrepreneurial model, in turn, is a role model for women who constitutes a source of knowledge about the entrepreneurial activity and an example to be followed or used by women as experience before creating their own enterprises. It provides her with courage to become an entrepreneur and allows her to obtain the necessary knowledge to develop the entrepreneurial activity.

5.   In spite of the predominance of the male domination in Latin American countries, women do not seem to note frustration with a male-dominated working environment or the need of a flexible schedule to attend family responsibilities as factors that influence their entrepreneurship. These gender-related factors do not seem to have an important influence in women entrepreneurs, even though they are frequently mentioned in the literature.

6.   Women have expressed that *achievement* and *autonomy* are the motives that seem to have more influence in entrepreneurship, while in a small proportion they have mentioned the motives of *power* and *affiliation*. Informant women entrepreneurs have expressed a high intrinsic motivation, in other words, they feel compelled to develop their enterprises due to a desire for achievement or an intrinsic reward that they find in their enterprises. The benefits sought by these women in their enterprises are not exclusively economic benefits. Thus, faced with the possibility of giving up their job and

live from their profits, they express that they prefer to continue working in search of further achievement and autonomy.

7.   Circumstances affecting entrepreneurship seem to show differences according to their demographic, educational and family background. Older women entrepreneurs seem to be more influenced by economic circumstances than by work or personal factors in their decision of choosing to become entrepreneurs. In younger women, work circumstances (such as the difficulty in finding a job, the lack of professional growth prospects or work frustration for economic reasons) seem to be more frequent.

8.   The group of women with a lower level of education seem to be more influenced by economic circumstances such as basic economic needs, insufficient family income or being frustrated because their work situation provides them with less income than they expect, in their decision to choose entrepreneurship. The group of women with a higher educational level seem to be more influenced by work circumstances such as frustration from a lack of professional development prospects or a belief that entrepreneurial activity is the logical continuation of their professional development.

9.   The group of women with more family responsibilities (dependent children) seem to be influenced in their decision to become entrepreneurs more by economic and family circumstances, which reinforces the evidence that, for women, the enterprise plays a part in their role within the family and is a way to fulfil that role by generating economic security for their children and relatives.

10.   It seems that women entrepreneurs cannot be considered a homogeneous group with unique characteristics, and that their profile must be expressed through a typology that represents their different experiences. Establishing a unique profile of women entrepreneurs that considers a sole dimension seems to be an inadequate simplification of their backgrounds. This chapter proposes a conceptual framework that explains the profile of women entrepreneurs from the stage of the work and personal life cycle during which they opt for entrepreneurship (since women start their enterprises at different moments of their life, and this affects the type of business and their particular approach to ownership

of the enterprise) and the factors that stimulated them to become entrepreneurs. Results have identified six profiles of women entrepreneurs that express different routes by which women achieve entrepreneurship: Young Women with Employment Options, Growing Women with External Constraints, Consolidated Women with a Truncated Career, Natural Young Women, Growing Women and Consolidated Professional Women.

Recommendations

1.   The establishment of national statistics on entrepreneurial activity is recommended, and particularly the collection of information on gender. These are currently scarce and contradictory, which limits knowledge on entrepreneurial activity, and particularly on women entrepreneurial activity.

2.   The establishment of a clear definition of the concept of *entrepreneurial activity* is recommended, differentiating it from *self-employment*. Self-employment may mean a way of living in view of economic need, but entrepreneurial implies an inclination towards the search of opportunities and resources for the development of a project. Many studies and policies do not distinguish self-employment from entrepreneurial activity, which produces confusion in their analysis.

3.   Although women represent an important and growing proportion of entrepreneurial activity, support programmes have been developed without a deep knowledge of the reality of women entrepreneurs. Women entrepreneurs seem not to constitute a homogeneous group and cannot be considered as a sole category. Women entrepreneurs apparently constitute a complex group and have diverse backgrounds, skills, circumstances and motives, and obstacles. Support programmes and policies should have a deep knowledge of women and be developed specifically for each type of women entrepreneurs.

4.   The existence of an entrepreneurial model, as well as support from people close to the entrepreneur, has appeared to be as an important pattern for entrepreneurial development. Thus, women

without a readily apparent entrepreneurial model should take advantage of a formal "mentoring entrepreneurs" programme, in which women entrepreneurs may offer their *mentoring* to women who are beginning their entrepreneurial activity. The purpose of such a programme is that the new entrepreneurs: (a) obtain security about their entrepreneurial orientation; (b) learn about the management of an enterprise; (c) obtain knowledge and guidance in the most deficient areas; and (d) develop more confidence in their own entrepreneurial capabilities.

5. Women entrepreneurs with work experience before becoming entrepreneurs are better prepared for the entrepreneurial activity than those with no experience. It is thus recommended that women gain work experience before starting an enterprise, as it will increase their confidence for decision making and enable them to learn how an enterprise works.

6. Programmes aimed at stimulating women entrepreneurship should consider the following areas: (a) advisory and consulting services; (b) training in business management; (c) financing; (d) access to information; and (e) a network of contacts. The purpose of advisory and consulting services is to study their skills, offer them support in starting their enterprises and plan and develop their enterprises. These services would deal with the specific problems faced by women entrepreneurs and give them a clear picture of the degree of dedication necessary to develop an enterprise and the capacity to balance their family and entrepreneurial responsibilities. Training aims at improving women's skills in business management by training them in specific topics and developing their capacity to raise the human capital necessary to promote their enterprises. With training, women should be able to acknowledge their own weaknesses and know how to hire the people they need for the areas they do not dominate. Access to financing should be facilitated, the system of guarantees required should be simplified and, most importantly, and the cost of credit for women (and men) entrepreneurs should be reduced. Access to information about markets, new products, business development and management should be facilitated, which will enable women to expand opportunities for their businesses. A network of contacts enables women to interchange experiences with entrepreneurs and

professional organizations and increase their opportunities to create enterprises, and is a useful source of inspiration. The network of contacts and the access to information expose women to a broader business environment and give them access to opportunities to realize their own potential as entrepreneurs.

References

Avolio, B. (2010). *A Profile of Women Entrepreneurship in Peru: An Exploratory Study*. Doctoral Thesis.

Carter, S. and Cannon, T. (1992). *Women as Entrepreneurs*. London: Academic Press.

Hisrich, R. and Brush, C. (1984). The women entrepreneur: Management and business problems. *Journal of Small Business Management, 22*(1), 30–37.

Hisrich, R. and Brush, C. (1986). *The Woman Entrepreneur: Starting, Financing and Managing a Successful New Business*. Toronto, Canada: Lexington Books, D.C. Heath and Company.

4

Female Entrepreneurship: Obstacles Faced by Women Entrepreneurs

Theoretical Background

In the United States and Canada, the problems that women suffer in their enterprises have been studied. An initial study by Schwartz (1976) of 20 women entrepreneurs in the United States identified the main problem at the moment of starting an enterprise as the discrimination in access to credit. Hisrich and O'Brien (1981) analysed demographic factors, motivations and problems of 21 women entrepreneurs in the United States and found that women have problems with the guarantees required to obtain a loan, and with the perception what women do not act in business as seriously as men.

In the United States, Hisrich and Brush (1986) found that the main problems pointed out by women entrepreneurs are their lack of training in business, difficulty in obtaining credit, weak position for obtaining collateral and lack of experience in financial planning. In the US State of Florida, Neider (1987) found that the two major women's problems were their lack the ability to delegate and the tension between their personal and working lives. Lee-Gosselin and Grisé (1990) studied 400 women enterprise owners/administrators in Quebec, Canada. They found that women could benefit from technical support, help from other entrepreneurs and other professionals such as bankers and accountants, and from a better understanding of the production process and the surrounding context at the beginning of enterprise's operations. They also explored the main obstacles women face when starting their business and found these to be the following: lack of confidence from banks, suppliers and customers; lack of capital to start their enterprise; and family obligations. Problems women face during the creation of their enterprises are: credibility before banks and suppliers, marketing problems and difficulties in recruiting and attracting competent personnel. However, they did not report financial problems, and a few of them pointed to their partners/ husbands as an obstacle. Most women felt that those obstacles were related to gender (Lee-Gosselin and Grisé, p. 427).

In Hungary, Hisrich and Fulop (1994) interviewed 50 women entrepreneurs about the difficulties when starting their enterprises. The three most frequently mentioned problems were: difficulty in obtaining loans, weak position for obtaining collateral and lack of experience in financial planning, and difficulties in conciliating the demands of their families and their enterprises. Men also face these problems, but social factors make them more difficult for women. For example, few women own property, which is the most common collateral requested by banks when applying for credit.

In addition, the most frequent problems are the lack of experience in hiring external services, legal problems and the lack of respect for women's enterprises. Other factors that affect only women, as quoted by Hisrich and Fulop (1994), are: a lack of mentors, an entrepreneurial culture with little respect for women entrepreneurs and the lack of training in entrepreneurial activities.

In Poland, Mroczkowski (1997) found that women entrepreneurs have more difficulty in combining their work and family responsibilities due to economic conditions (less income, less resources and less free time) and to the prevalence of stereotypes of gender roles. In Turkey, the most frequent problem was the lack of relationships with other entrepreneurs, the lack of managerial experience and the lack of experience in hiring external services (Hisrich and Ayse Öztürk, 1999).

Obstacles Faced by Women Entrepreneurs

The methodology described in Chapter 2 explored the principal obstacles women entrepreneurs face in starting their enterprises and making them grow. The obstacles found arose from the testimony of the women and have been compared with those considered in literature. The results show that there is no unique experience among women entrepreneurs, but that women experience common obstacles. The obstacles identified in the study have been categorized as: (a) those related to the gender of the entrepreneur; and (b) those related to the entrepreneurial activity and not directly related to the gender of the entrepreneur (Table 4.1).

Table 4.1   Matrix of obstacles faced by women entrepreneurs (n=24)

Obstacles	A	B	C	D	E	F	G	H	I	J	K	L	M	N	O	P	Q	R	S	T	U	V	W	X
Family responsibilities	X	X	X	X			X			X		X									X	X		X
Discrimination in access to credit									X											X				X
Difficulties in obtaining financing										X								X	X					X
Afraid of becoming indebted						X	X		X			X												
Lack of loan guarantees											X	X			X	X								
Lack of education in business management						X		X		X				X			X		X					
Lack of experience in financial planning												X			X				X	X				
Lack of self-confidence				X						X	X													
Husband/partner as obstacle				X								X												
Hiring of competent personnel				X																		X		
Lack of work experience																					X			

The obstacles expressed by women entrepreneurs that are related to gender are: (a) the difficulty to conciliate family and entrepreneurial responsibilities, since women have primary responsibilities for their children and the house, while men spend most of their time in their own work activities; and (b) discriminatory conditions in the access to financing, mainly in the requirements to obtain loans (Avolio, 2010).

Consideration of the relationship between the obstacles indicated by women and their backgrounds, shows that: (a) women present a lack of education in business management, regardless of their educational level, even those with university education; (b) the difficulty to reconcile entrepreneurial and family responsibilities is related to a woman's number of children, the age of her children and her level of responsibility in the household (whether she has support from her husband/partner). The smaller the children, the more difficult it is to reconcile work and family responsibilities. Evidently, there is more difficulty when the woman does not have the support of her husband/partner and she assumes all the household responsibility (Avolio, 2010).

The obstacle of family responsibilities is consistent with MITINCI (1997) studies, which indicate that women consider the housework to be their responsibility whilst they also have an economically productive job. On the one hand, women worry about neglecting their children and the household, but on the other hand, they also need to obtain income for the family. That is why women feel compelled to adequately perform both roles simultaneously (MITINCI, 1997). It is important to point out that this obstacle is not confined to the women's entrepreneurial activity, but is related to the work activity of women in general.

The obstacles faced by women that are unrelated to gender are: (a) difficulties related to the guarantees required to obtain a loan; (b) fear of debts; (c) a weak position of obtain collaterals for the loans; (d) lack of education in business administration, which limits them in the development of their enterprises; (e) lack of experience in financial planning; (f) limitations that women impose on themselves due to a lack of confidence in their entrepreneurial capabilities; and, less frequently (g) a negative attitude by their husbands/partners; (h) difficulty in hiring competent personnel; and (i) a lack of work experience (Avolio, 2010).

The way women entrepreneurs face their lack of education in business administration has implications in their management style and, eventually, in the composition of the ownership of the enterprise. In individual enterprises, where women clearly perceive this obstacle (as in the cases of Teresa San Borja, Jesusa Rímac and Enit Moyobamba), they lean on external services or hire such services. In other cases, when women are not conscious of this obstacle, they incorporate a partner with administrative skills into their enterprises to compensate for their lack of education. In the first case, hiring persons with the management skills they don't have permits the organization to grow over time. In the second case, incorporating a partner with management skills has implications in the development of the enterprise, which is limited by that person's management capacity (Avolio, 2010).

No women reported the lack of a network of contacts or a male-dominated entrepreneurial environment as an obstacle, both of which have been mentioned in literature. A male-dominated entrepreneurial environment may be expressed in a perception that women-owned enterprises are less trustworthy, more risky and less serious than men-owned ones; that they present barriers to making decisions; and/or limit access to the circles of power in the countries. The results show that women entrepreneurs do not seem to have felt limited by a male-dominated entrepreneurial environment, which does not mean that it does not exist, but that they do not perceive it as an important obstacle in their entrepreneurial activity (Avolio, 2010).

These results are consistent with previous research on the principal obstacles women entrepreneurs face in their enterprises. In the United States and Canada, the principal obstacles indicated by women are: discrimination in access to credit; problems with the guarantees needed to obtain a credit; the perception that women do not act as seriously as men in business; the lack of confidence from the banks, suppliers and customers; tensions between their personal and working lives; a lack of training in business management; a lack of experience in financial planning; a lack of skill in delegating authority; a lack of capital to start the enterprise; marketing problems; and difficulties in recruiting and attracting competent personnel (Hisrich and Brush, 1986; Hisrich and O'Brien, 1981; Lee-Gosselin and Grisé, 1990; Neider, 1987; Schwartz, 1976). In Hungary, the most frequent problems women pointed out were: difficulty obtaining credit, including a lack of property to act as loan guarantees; difficulty in reconciling the demands of the enterprise with those of the family; lack of experience in hiring external services; legal problems; lack of mentors; an entrepreneurial culture lacking respect towards women entrepreneurs; and the lack of training in business management (Hisrich and Fulop, 1994). In Turkey, the most frequent problems in starting an enterprise are: financial; obtaining loans; lack of guidance and advice; lack of relationships with other entrepreneurs; lack of managerial experience, and inexperience in hiring external services (Hisrich and Ayse Öztürk, 1999).

Next, the obstacles that are apparent from the testimony of the entrepreneurs are explained in detail:

Family Responsibilities

Family responsibilities present a difficulty for women's entrepreneurial development, since they have to be capable of reconciling their family and personal responsibilities, while men tend to devote most of their time to their profession. Ten women interviewed for the study expressed that they face difficulties reconciling their diverse roles:

> How does being a mother influence in your enterprise? It takes time away … if I had more time, my business would grow more. (Monica 129:132)

> Have you had problems to balance your family responsibilities with your daughters and your enterprise? That is the problem, in that aspect the man is freer, while the woman is more tied to housework; you can't give your children the time you really want to. When you work somewhere else, you have a stable time to go home, but here I stay as long as I can. (Rosaluz 68:68)

> The biggest obstacle is your children's time … to take care of my children and devote myself to my job. (Marcelina 117:117)

Financing

Financing is an obstacle that women have expressed from several perspectives. Some perceive discrimination in access to financing as an obstacle, when financial institutions demand the economic guarantee of the husband/partner as one of the requirements to get a loan, while this doesn't happen the other way around. Other women expressed fear of receiving financing and becoming indebted, and some have experienced difficulties in obtaining financing because of the guarantees required (property deeds, collateral). This difficulty is frequently pointed out by the microenterprise and small enterprise sector in

the country, due to the high level of informality in real estate property deeds, which prevents the use of their properties as collateral.

Two women in the study expressed that they felt discriminated against in their efforts to gain access to credit; four women expressed having difficulties in obtaining financing; four women expressed their fear of becoming indebted; and four women expressed having problems with the guarantees required for financing. These include Gloria, Liliana, Monica and Carmela:

> *Here machismo and gender are still predominant; here men still have a little more dominance ... when you go to the bank and they say "Tell me ma'am, who is your husband? What does your husband do? Your husband has to come to sign this, and your husband has to bring his identification document." But if your husband asks for a loan, they don't ask for his wife to go sign any papers or anything. (Gloria 653:655)*

> *If a man goes to the bank, they don't ask him if he's married and don't ask him for his wife's documents, nothing. The man, because he is male, fills out his own papers, his own documents. Marital status is irrelevant. (Gloria 355:357)*

> *Have you had bank loans? Sometimes, but really small ones. Why very small ones? Because I haven't needed more. I am frightened of owing to the bank or to anyone. (Liliana 159:162)*

Lack of Education in Business Management

The lack of education in business management, mainly in financial, tax and accounting aspects, is an obstacle that women frequently point out. Six women indicated that the main difficulty in operating their enterprises was the lack of preparation in business management, and four women expressed having difficulties dealing with financial topics:

> *Which have been the biggest challenges to start and operate your enterprise? Not knowing anything about businesses. I mean, I really started this to do what I wanted and earn money. The hardest thing was, really, working with an accountant. Working with the lawyer. I mean, everything else was a problem. (Teresa 243:244)*

If you could go back in time, what would you have studied or what training would you have chosen as something useful for you to start your enterprise? I would have studied something that would have helped the enterprise. (Liliana 8:14)

Lack of Self-confidence

In some cases, a lack of self-confidence is an obstacle for women, who may have doubts about their own capacities or about the success of their businesses. These doubts make them take precautionary measures or postpone the start-up of their enterprises until they feel sure of their capacities. Three women expressed this as an obstacle to the development of their enterprises:

I wanted to try myself, because I wasn't sure of what I knew, if I could perform as well or better in the other place; that's why I went to work with that lady, but with permission from the other place. I hadn't told my boss I was quitting; I told him I was going to my hometown. What I wanted was to try. (Ruth 65:65)

The Husband/Partner

Though many women consider their partners to be a support in their enterprises, two women indicated that he represented an obstacle for their entrepreneurial development:

It was like having another son ... He was supposed to know how it all worked, since he had seen me handling the business for so long ... the business lasted four months, then it all went downhill, I even ended up at the police station since the debts he had were exaggerated. He had to pay for the apartment, the place I had rented; he didn't pay for electricity or water services, he had debts on beer and all that ... I already wanted to work, I started working with the kids, and he came to see the children, and he told them something like "Your Mom makes you work too much, like slaves." He put ideas in their heads, until I forbade him to come, it was too much. (Ruth 106:106)

Conclusions

Studies in the United States and Canada show that the most important obstacles reported by women entrepreneurs for the development of their enterprises are: discrimination in access to credit; problems with the guarantees needed to obtain a credit; the perception that women do not act as seriously as men in business; the lack of confidence from the banks, suppliers and customers; tensions between their personal and working lives; a lack of training in business management; a lack of experience in financial planning; a lack of skill in delegating authority; a lack of capital to start the enterprise; marketing problems; and difficulties in recruiting and attracting competent personnel: (Hisrich and O'Brien, 1981; Lee-Gosselin and Grisé, 1990; Hisrich and Brush, 1986; Neider, 1987; Schwartz, 1976).

In Hungary, the most common problems that women reported were: difficulty obtaining credit, including a lack of property to act as loan guarantees; difficulty in reconciling the demands of the enterprise with those of the family; lack of experience in hiring external services; legal problems; lack of mentors; an entrepreneurial culture lacking respect towards women entrepreneurs; and the lack of training in business management (Hisrich and Fulop, 1994). In Turkey, to some extent, the most common problems in starting an enterprise are: financial; obtaining loans; lack of guidance and advice; lack of relationships with other entrepreneurs; lack of management experience; and inexperience in the employment of external services (Hisrich and Ayse Öztürk, 1999).

The main obstacles that women seem to face are related to entrepreneurial activity in general, and are not specific to their gender. However, some social factors make these obstacles appear to be greater for women (such as the fact that few women are the sole proprietors of real estate, the most common collateral requested by banks when applying for a loan; or that, in a culture where women are responsible for taking care of the house and children, they must combine their responsibilities at home and at work).

The main gender-specific obstacle that women entrepreneurs seem to face is the traditional division of roles at home that places the main responsibility in taking care of the children and the house on women at the same time that they perform economically productive work. This is due to the strong cultural patterns on the role of women in society (Avolio, 2010). These demands on the women entrepreneur to care for the house to a larger measure than men require her to perform several tasks simultaneously and create stress in the use of her time or a conflict between her roles as mother and entrepreneur. To decrease this obstacle, it is necessary to redefine the female role in the family, in other words, to maintain a better balance in the couple with respect to responsibilities at home.

The main obstacles women entrepreneurs seem to face that are not related to their gender are: financing; lack of education to manage enterprises; limitations imposed on themselves due to a lack of confidence in their own capacities; the attitude of their husbands/partners; difficulty in hiring skilled personnel; and the lack of work experience. No woman reported financial problems, the lack of a network of contacts or the existence of a male-dominated entrepreneurial environment to be an obstacle, although these obstacles are found in other studies.

The way women entrepreneurs face their lack of training to manage enterprises seems to impact their management style and, eventually, the composition of the ownership of the enterprise. The creation of support programmes aimed at training in enterprise management and business advisory services may help to reduce these obstacles. The objective of these support programmes should not be training experts in all areas, but the development of a business management capacity through the knowledge of several aspects that must be taken into account for the development of the enterprise. Thus, future women entrepreneurs may identify which of these aspects require hiring collaborators or external advisory services, and do not become dependent on partners or relatives for the development of their enterprises.

References

Avolio, B. (2010). *A Profile of Women Entrepreneurship in Peru: An Exploratory Study*. Doctoral Thesis.

Hisrich, R. (1986). The woman entrepreneur: a comparative analysis. *Leadership and Organization Development Journal*, 7(2), 8–16.

Hisrich, R. and Ayse Öztürk, S. (1999). Women entrepreneurs in a developing economy. *Journal of Management Development*, 38(2), 114–124.

Hisrich, R. and Brush, C. (1986). *The Woman Wntrepreneur: Starting, Financing and Managing a successful new business*. Toronto, Canada: Lexington Books, D.C. Heath and Company.

Hisrich, R. and Fulop, G. (1994). The role of women entrepreneurs in Hungary's transition economy. *International Studies of Management and Organization*, 24(4), 100–118.

Hisrich, R. and O'Brien, M. (1981). The woman entrepreneur from a business and sociological perspective. In Vesper, K.H. (Ed.), *Frontiers on Entrepreneurship Research* (pp. 21–39). Wellesley, MA: Babson College Center for Entrepreneurship.

Lee-Gosselin, H. and Grisé, J. (1990). Are women owner-managers challenging our definitions of entrepreneurship? An in-depth survey. *Journal of Business Ethics*, 9(4), 423–433.

Ministerio de Industria, Turismo, Integración y Negociaciones Comerciales Internacionales (MITINCI). (1997). *Desarrollando la perspectiva de genero en los centros de servicio empresarial*. Lima, Perú: Fondo para la equidad del género, DESIDE, COSUDE.

Mroczkowski, T. (1997). Women as employees and entrepreneurs in the Polish transformation. *Industrial Relations Journal*, 28(2), 83–91.

Neider, L. (1987). A preliminary investigation of female entrepreneurs in Florida. *Journal of Small Business Management*, 25(3), 22–28.

Schwartz, E. (1976). Entrepreneurship: A new female frontier. *Journal of Contemporary Business*, 5, 47–76.

5

Mumpreneurs

Introduction

According to the article entitled "Historical Evolution of Female and Social Gender Roles" in the 1920s, "socialization tools such as women's magazines promoted that a fulfilling life requires marriage, children and a career" (Volkert, 2008). Today, the traditional family model still requires a woman to maintain her family life while also keeping up with her career, but that a woman's family comes first. Although, as the article stated, some women are "opposed to fusing the two worlds", today, more women accept the coexistence of the two worlds, and some actually insist on it.

Because of today's weak economy, some women feel as if they must maintain "roles that are appropriate to the dire situation", just as women felt during the Great Depression. Thus, they feel as if they have to maintain a career, as their husband does, in order to support the household due to the fact that neither person is bringing in a sufficient income because of the poor economy. The traditional female role is very beneficial for the creation and development of new businesses by *mumpreneurs*.

In "Baby Einstein: Genius Through Imperfection" mumpreneur Julie Aigner Clark explains: "I've always been fortunate enough to do what I really love, that I feel really committed to and that involved my life as a mom … My businesses are great because they've revolved around my life as a mom" (Sherman, 2010). Sherman (2008) also writes that Aigner Carter's second business consisted of producing videos about children's safety issues that she wished existed for her own kids. This is not uncommon; inspiration for a large number of entrepreneurs' business ideas comes from raising children. Ideas for strollers, diapers, toys, learning activities, dolls and so on come from parents who realize there is a market need for something they wish existed. For example, Ruth Handler, the creator of the Barbie doll, came up with the idea for an "adult" doll after watching her daughter.

What is a Mumpreneur?

The term mumpreneur makes us think of a woman who has the best of both worlds: her own family and her own business, and is successful with each. In short, a mumpreneur is a woman who is determined to follow all of her dreams. Running a business is similar in some respects to running a household, which is why women, mothers in particular, are more inclined to start their own company. The responsibilities of running a household are endless, and they include taking care of children, paying bills, organizing and planning. In the business world, entrepreneurs are responsible for taking care of their team members, as well as paying bills, organizing and planning too. If women are able to excel at being in charge of their family, there is no reason why they cannot apply those skills to a business venture they would enjoy pursuing. These women must also be innovative, and entrepreneurs must be creative in order to think of what is needed to build a business and how to make that business more appealing than the competition.

Although women are entering careers that are "non-traditional", these types of skills will still be used to create businesses because people commonly use what they know best and are very good at when they create businesses. Currently, there are less differences in how men and women are raised, but there are still gender-specific traits that parents will teach their child; for example, more parents will teach their girls to sew and bake than they will to their boys.

A New Model for Doing Business

In our opinion, conditions have changed so drastically for women since the 1920s, from fighting for the right to vote and going to work in the factories during the Second World War, to the feminist revolution in the 1960s and 1970s. Gender roles are changing at work and at home, according to research the Families and Work Institute released in March 2009 (Galinsky, Aumann and Bond, 2009). Young men and women alike are challenging traditional gender roles and expecting to share in paid work as well as tending the household and children, according to this benchmark survey of 3,500 Americans.

A new generation of mums is creating a new model for doing business. Today mumpreneurs are very prominent because many women wish to have a family and children, but also have the dream of starting a business. They have a chance for the best of both worlds – private and professional. Many mumpreneurs are very successful women with home-based businesses who contribute an estimated three trillion dollars a year to the United States economy and create 23 million jobs (Palmer, 2010).

One of the strengths of a mum-run business lies in multitasking and working under pressure, which are definitely qualities of being a mum. Most mums know multitasking from taking care of their children. This is especially important for a mum running a business, because she will have to learn how to balance her personal and professional lives. A mumpreneur hopes to avoid long business meetings, boss's criticisms, should she be late for work, and so on.

However, although working from home allows for more freedom and different opportunities for quality time, still business owners fall into traps. Some lack organizational capabilities and fail to structure their commitments and time. Caring for family and raising children and running a business at the same time are two serious jobs which require full-time engagement. Therefore, the everyday schema of commitments is easily overloaded with numerous activities.

Numerous problems and frequent mistakes appear that may reflect negatively on overall business success. Among the most frequent are:

FAMILY CONFLICTS

Family conflicts are a frequent phenomenon because of an inability to balance family and professional commitments, which often lacks understanding by family members. When someone works at home, for example, their working space is close to other rooms where other members of the family spend their time, which may be a problem for both sides. These conflicts will be smaller if there is family harmony and understanding among all family members. A home business owner should explain to family members that (if they are not involved in the business themselves) during the day, some time must be dedicated solely to professional matters. The family must agree that the owner will be working longer than normal working hours during the first phase of the business. After that initial phase, which is always the toughest for any business owner, working hours may be gradually shortened, or outside help may be obtained. It is extremely important not to ignore this issue. If ignored, this can cause even greater problems for both the business and family.

ORGANIZATIONAL PROBLEMS

Many entrepreneurs who opt for working from home have problems organizing themselves. Considering that they often mix private with professional commitments, they make one of the biggest mistakes in running a home business. This can be explained by the fact that being one's own boss is a lot more difficult than it may seem. Many lack experience of running a business individually and, for some, it is their first time and therefore, they use their time irrationally and have a lot of idle time.

INSUFFICIENT ATTENTION TO MARKETING

For some, the importance of a strategy vis-à-vis the competition is not taken into account. Many home business owners fail to see the necessity in paying attention to customers' perceptions of their businesses compared to the competition (Radović-Marković and Silver Kyaruzi, 2010). Problems may arise due to the lack of marketing information, thus a periodical market analysis is recommended. This analysis should provide the company with the information necessary for its target market.

New Market Expansion Possibilities for Small Home Businesses

Considering that the aging population trend is present in many countries, one could rightfully ask a question about the increase in this market segment, which will have a great share in total market demand. That is, how is this growth going to change the business environment? Since the population is getting old, it will have different spending and saving habits during different phases of their lives. The needs of seniors are significantly different from middle-aged or young people's needs. In view of this, senior citizens have less need for savings than the younger ones, which is reflected in the increase in their spending. A business opportunity can be found here for the mum entrepreneurs performing their work at home for the senior citizens, such as the provision of health care services, food preparation and distribution to old and ill persons, the provision of a variety of information and advice and preparation of different cultural and other programmes, among others.

Conclusions

Society has evolved and has accepted the presence of women in the workplace more than the past. Women, nowadays, tend to look at having a career as a crucial part of their self-fulfillment. Women's roles in history vary from being the nurse to a household mother: regardless of their job description, they have all contributed a great deal. When the topic of business is considered, women seem to be using their niche to develop business ideas. Many mumpreneurs have their own accounting firms, Ebay accounts, and even become private consultants in order to be close to the family and still have the career. There is one specific approach of women towards business selection. Namely, most women would rather pursue something they are passionate about rather than an appealing market opportunity, except those who are purely entrepreneurial and money-oriented. In addition, we can see that many companies are adopting this concept of work at home mum. Furthermore, many companies can hire these mum entrepreneurs to work from their homes and so, decrease their cost in office space since their partners work remotely.

References

Galinsky, E., Aumann, K. and Bond, J. (2009). *Times are changing.* Families and Work Institute. Retrieved August 2011 from http://workingmoms.about.com/od/workingmomsresearch/a/GenderRoles.htm.

Palmer, K. (27 April 2010). *Behind the "Mompreneur" myth.* Retrieved 25 June 2012 from http://money.usnews.com/money/personal-finance/articles/2010/04/27/behind-the-mompreneur-myth.

Radović-Marković, M. (2009). *Women Entrepreneurs: New Opportunities and Challenges* Delhi, India: Indo-American Books.

Radović-Marković, M. and Silver Kyaruzi, I. (2010). *Women in Business: Theory, Practice and Flexible Approaches.* London: Adonis and Abbey.

Sherman, A. (8 May 2008). *What's a mompreneur … really?* http://shine.yahoo.com/work-money/whats-a-mompreneur-really-167496.html.

Sherman, A. (8 July 2010). *Baby Einstein: Genius through imperfection.* http://www.entrepreneur.com/startingabusiness/mompreneur/article207318.html.

Volkert, F. (21 January 2008). *Historical evolution of female and social gender roles.* Retrieved from http://voices.yahoo.com/historical-evolution-female-social-gender-roles-822575.html.

6

Women and Inequality Problems

Introduction

In this chapter we are concerned with the past and current processes of economic and social transformation of the role of women. In this context, it is necessary to stress that the battle for women's rights started back in the late eighteenth century, which set the stage for the rise of women's movements (Radović-Marković, 2009). The traditional thinking was the common cliché that a woman's place was in the kitchen, and that a woman's job was to clean the house, look after the children and wash the dishes. They were given undistinguished and low-status functions, and for the most part, were denied any real opportunity to show their true talents.

To explore these facts, we draw primarily upon our experience while editing a volume of essays entitled *The Perspective of Women's Entrepreneurship in the Age of Globalization* (Radović-Marković, 2007). They are often excluded when it comes to promotions and disrespected within the employment hierarchy. Women almost always work in the informal sector in developing countries. Namely, in the informal sector women work longer hours and are paid on average 25 per cent less than men, but have made significant gains in entering formerly male-dominated jobs in the labour force. The majority of women in developing countries lack social protection and economic safety nets, thus they are easily exploited in terms of wages and working hours.

Nonetheless, much research is still oriented towards men and their problems. A feminist perspective requires the evaluation of literature from the standpoint of the presentation of women. A large number of studies point out that income disparities increase in the early stages of development, making the poor relatively worse off. Some studies deny the existence of the inverse relation between equality of income and economic growth (Buedo, 2002) and some give evidence of the negative impact of inequality and the positive effect of redistribution upon growth (Aghion et al., 1999).

Although it is widely accepted that inequality problems are best solved by rapid economic development, the predominant opinion in modern literature is that ignoring inequality in the pursuit of development can also be perilous (Jovičić and Milojević, 2010). Some authors have argued that inequality has risen further in those countries that actively pursued reforms (see, for example, Milanović, 1998). There is also empirical evidence of a significant direct link between the level of income inequality and the share of the economy held by the informal sector. Rutkowski (1996) highlighted the fact that the exclusion of the informal sector in the transition countries, where it accounts for a significant part of overall economic activity, is likely to underestimate the actual level of earnings inequality. Spariosu (2007) concluded that inequality and the growth of the informal economy in the early stage of the transition process can be interpreted as a result of the general decrease of economic activities caused by the major transition processes of: reallocation and restructuring. However, in our opinion, the emergence and the development of the informal economy is a consequence of disorganization.

Women's Right to Employment

A recent United Nations report indicated that economic development is closely related to the advancement of women. For instance, in nations where women have advanced, economic growth has usually been steady. By contrast, in countries where women have been restricted, the economy has been stagnant. Statistical data and information on the situation of transitional countries shows difficulties faced by women in the science sector. The stereotypical image of scientists is male. Namely, women still constitute a minority of researchers in Europe, but this is even more so in technological research and in the business–enterprise sector (Radović-Marković, 2011).

Having read some scientific articles written by Afgan and Carvalho (2010), I have come to the conclusion that one cannot talk about human rights and leave out the problem of women's position in society and their right to employment. This issue has to be given special attention keeping in mind that the problem of discrimination in both employment of women in the labour force and in their promotion at work is still far from being solved. Namely, women who have successfully joined the modern work force have not been fairly rewarded for usually being paid less for their work than their male counterparts at the same job level. Women earn on average 15 per cent less than men in the European Union (EU) (Radović-Marković, 2009).

A similar problem is with the low representation of women in upper executive positions (32 per cent) regardless of the fact that they, on average, are higher educated than men. Further concern is seen in the fact that this percentage increased by only 1 per cent during the last five years. In Germany, for example, women earn on average 22 per cent per hour less than men. For this reason, Germany is the EU country with the largest gap in incomes between the genders. Only women in Estonia, Cyprus and Slovakia earn an average income as high as or higher than men. One reason in Germany for such differences is that a large number of women there work only half of the standard number of working hours. In this regard, the European Commission requires better solutions to achieve harmonization between family and work, and to increase the number of women in upper executive positions (Radović-Marković, 2011).

According to reports of the European Commission, the employment of women has been constantly increasing during the past few years. One in three women works part time, while only 8 per cent of men are employed in this way. The employment rate for women with children is 62 per cent, while for men it is as high as 91 per cent. In the transition countries of Central and Eastern Europe, women have adverse economic status due to their having a reduced number of employees in the public sector, a higher rate of unemployment, greater job insecurity and a poor system of social protection (Radović-Marković, 2011). They are often excluded when it comes to promotions and disrespected within the employment hierarchy. Additionally, they were given undistinguished and low-status functions, and for the most part, denied any real opportunity to show their true talents. Women's role in the business world has been unjustly marginalized in many countries worldwide, which diminished their abilities to creatively participate in business decision making within their companies.

Informality and Gender Aspects

In addition, three approaches to the informal economy can be distinguished: the direct approach, the indirect or discrepancy approach and the model approach. The first two approaches are based on a single factor as the main generator of the informal economy. However, the informal economy is a complex phenomenon determined by many factors. Consequently, in the most advanced model approach, the multiple causes and indicators are treated simultaneously and explicitly as the determinants of the informal economy.

This sector is especially important for the transition countries and the developing countries where more than one-third of the labour force is employed in this sector of economy. In the transition economies and in the developing countries, informal work emerges primarily for survival purposes, while in the developed countries it spreads from opportunities. In the majority of the transition economies, in fact, those employed in the informal sector are not protected by law (Radović-Marković, 2011).

The high rate of unemployment, low wages and non-payment of salaries has led to the rapid growth of informal employment. Examples of informal work in Eastern Europe are multiple job holdings that combine employment in what remains of the public sector (for example, teachers and doctors) with other activities because of low purchasing power. The informal economy, or residual economy, may take different forms, and it consists of a range of informal enterprises and informal jobs. Jobs in informal sector are at first sight invisible, for example, hotel jobs, restaurant jobs, jobs in major cities' streets (fruit and vegetables salesmen and saleswomen, refreshing drinks salespersons, and so on).

In Eastern Europe, we especially have in mind the unfavourable conditions of work and long working hours, as well as the reward system and pay for the job accomplished. Public assistance is also missing – there are no special-purpose loans or credits, further preventing women from implementing their entrepreneurial and managerial potentials. Improvement of the working and living conditions of the informal sector labour force, which does not participate in business decision making because it includes mainly low-skilled labour force, requires their education and training. The end result should be their inclusion into the formal sector of economy, where they would be entitled to all the legal rights observed in the legal employment.

The gender analysis of the informal economy should not be restricted to the identification of differences between men and women; it also involves dimensions that intervene in social relations from which adjustments are to be made to the policies and institutions in order to reach goals of fairness. Still there are many companies that do not acknowledge that women can do a job as well as men, and there are many limiting, sexist and chauvinistic views on women running some businesses. Therefore, in many countries women grow increasingly dissatisfied with these limitations. The main problems with the employment of women are as follows: age discrimination, inadequate qualification structure and, pressures to delay marriage and parenthood

(Radović-Marković, 2009). Providing women with increased economic opportunity for employment is critical to the challenges faced by the world economies.

Age Discrimination in Employment and Gender

Age discrimination in employment refers to the use of "crude proxies" in personnel decisions, related to hiring, promotion, retraining, firing and mandatory retirement (MacNicol, 2006). The negative consequences of age discrimination in employment can include barriers to recruitment and hiring, diminished conditions of work and employment, limited career development and, in the absence of legislation, diminished employment protections and rights (Ghosheh, 2008). Recent literature cites that age discrimination occurs when preferences are based on age, rather than on an individual's merit, credentials or job performance (Cohen and Tsui, 1996; Guillemard et al., 1994; Ngo et al., 2002; Riger and Galligan, 1980) and pointed out noticeable socio-psychological and physiological differences within age discrimination. Age discrimination is a moral issue as well as a personal one but it's also a serious issue for businesses (Wilson, 2006). Research suggests that employers' attitudes towards older workers are frequently related to misconceptions concerning older workers' abilities (American Association for Retired Persons, 1994). A frequent accusation against older applicants is that they are less mentally flexible and less physically active than their youthful competitors (Riach and Rich, 2006). Specifically, employers judge older workers to be in poor health, resistant to change, uncreative, prone to accidents, disinterested in technological change and hard to train (Guillemard et al., 1994).

Furthermore, employers' attitudes towards older workers vary significantly according to the company's size, the employer's age, and gender, with older, female employers from smaller companies displaying the most positive attitudes (Berger, 1999). Until recently, research into the redundancy and job search experiences of older workers focused primarily on early retirement and exit of male workers, and tended to neglect the experiences of older women (Duncan, 2003). Research also suggests that older women are frequently perceived as both less attractive and less competent than younger women (Itzin and Phillipson, 1993; Loretto et al., 2000).

The importance of appearance in seeking or maintaining employment, particularly for females, has been noted in the literature: "When women attain the symbolic meaning of 'physically unattractive' (to men) they may be pushed out of visible areas or forced into retirement regardless of their skills" (Reinharz, 1986).

Women who have chosen clerical, secretarial or reception work may be especially liable to discrimination during the latter part of their working lives, as they work in female-dominated occupations where ageism and sexism frequently combine to create the "double jeopardy" of "gendered ageism" (Onyx, 1998). In countries when unemployment is low, and fewer applicants are searching for work, employers have less opportunity to discard applicants on the basis of some arbitrary characteristic such as gender and age (Riach and Rich, 2002).

As many scholars have pointed out (Gordon, 1996; Horn, 1994; Robertson, 1998; Roos and Gladwin, 2000), male-orientated ideologies often prevent adequate recognition of female contributions and, in some instances, do limit their participation. In some countries, women are subjected to negative stereotypes that, in turn, lead to them being deprived of resources (Hill and Macan, 1996), thus forcing them into the informal sector. The World Conference on Ageing held in Madrid in 2002 endorsed a life course approach to well-being in old age which is especially important for women "as they face obstacles throughout life with a cumulative effect on their social, economic, physical and psychological well-being in their later years" (United Nations, 2002).

Those older women who grew up when the male career model predominated may be particularly vulnerable to the effects of gendered ageism within the workplace. Such women were often socialized into leaving school with limited qualifications, entering traditionally female occupations and either withdrawing from the labour force or working part time while their children were young (Handy and Davy, 2005). However, the finding from more than 100 investigations is that there is no significant difference between the job performance of men and women, older and younger workers (Warr, 1994). In this context, some labour market economists are already beginning to re-examine their assumptions that the preference for younger workers is economically rational (Lazear, 1995).

Despite there being considerable literature in the area of age discrimination, limited research has been conducted in age discrimination in employment against older adults between the ages of 55 and 64. In addition, there has been little, if any, consideration of the quality of jobs and working conditions in policy discussions surrounding extending the legal working age (Ghosheh, 2008).

European Gender Equality Policies

Gender equality is a fundamental right and a necessary condition for all countries in achieving the EU's objectives of growth, employment and social cohesion. Equal participation of women and men in decision making symbolizes the level of political maturity of societies. Analyses show that in transition countries, the economic position of women deteriorates as a consequence of coexistence of various factors, These include: tradition and patriarchy being widespread in society; the fall in purchasing power and, the diminished role of the State, the shrinking of the public sector, budget restrictions that especially affect women since health care, education and other benefits decrease along with their rights to maternity leave, child care and pensions. The decrease in employment rates and the rise in unemployment rates; the rise in the share of women among the poor (feminization of poverty); the growth of the black market economy, which stimulates exploitation and discrimination of women; insufficient transparency of the privatization process that shuts out most women; absence of the practice of gender budgeting, making economic discrimination of women at a macroeconomic level invisible; conflict of roles (family and work), the burden of which is still predominantly on women's shoulders.

Sustainable development is possible when gender equality and economic development go hand in hand. Otherwise, we deal with an unbalanced development. In the process of promoting and implementing policies of gender equality and empowerment of women, non-governmental organizations (NGOs) and networks play an important role. Their actions and advocacy of public policy affect the public by proposing and solving particular problems. Strengthening civil society is a permanent goal and an imperative prerequisite for an advanced society in the field of human rights for women, which is extremely important to further improving the system of cooperation, coordination and partnership of NGOs with governmental institutions at both the national and the local levels.

Although, in recent years, EU policy has been oriented towards establishing the institutional framework and the promotion of inclusion principles of gender equality in different areas of policy within and outside the Union, it is evident that it is necessary to continue work on strengthening these institutions and forms for cooperation through unified activity towards a more effective enforcement of legislation and implementation of the EU and national policy goals.

Conclusions

Throughout history, women have fallen into certain social and societal roles. Although these have changed dramatically in the last century, certain stereotypes still apply. The gender analysis of the informal economy, as well as age discrimination in employment, should not be restricted to the identification of differences between men and women; it also involves dimensions that intervene in social relations from which adjustments are to be made to the policies and institutions in order to reach goals of fairness (Radović-Marković, 2009).

All the above requires new concepts that will enable us to reframe theories, in order to see gender issues in new ways and gain new insights.

References

Afgan, N.H. and Carvalho, M.G. (2010). The knowledge society: A sustainability paradigm. *Cadmus, 1*(1), 28–41.

Aghion, P., Caroli, E. and García-Peñalosa, C. (1999). Inequality and economic growth: The perspective of the new growth theories. *Journal of Economic Literature, 37*(4), 1615–1660.

American Association for Retired Persons (1994). *How to Manage Older Workers.* Washington DC: American Association of Retired Persons.

Berger, E.D. (1999). *Organizational and personal characteristics influencing Canadian employers' attitudes toward older workers* (MSc dissertation, University of Toronto, 1999).

Buedo, J. (2002). *The Trade-off between Efficiency and Equality: The Role of a Changing Economic Idea in the Political Strategy of the Social Democracy,* EUI Working paper 5. European Union Institute, Florence.

Cohen, A.G. and Tsui, A. (1996). Reactions to perceived discrimination. *Human Relations, 49,* 791–813.

Duncan, C. (2003). Assessing anti-ageism routes to older worker re-engagement. *Work, Employment and Society, 17*(1), 101–120.

Ghosheh, N. (2008). *Age discrimination and older workers: Theory and legislation in comparative context* (Conditions of Work and Employment Series No 20). Geneva, Switzerland: ILO.

Gordon, A. (1996). *Transforming Capitalism and Patriarchy: Gender and Development in Africa.* Boulder, CO: Lynne Reimer.

Guillemard, A.M., Gutek, B.A. and Walker, A. (1994). *Employers' responses to workforce ageing: A comparative Franco-British exploration*. Paris and Sheffield: University of Paris and Department of Sociological Studies, University of Sheffield.

Handy, J. and Davy, D. (2005). *Reproducing gendered ageism: Interpreting the interactions between mature female job-seekers and employment agency staff*. Presented at Fifth International Critical Management Studies Conference, July, Manchester, UK.

Hill, R.P. and Macan, S. (1996). Consumer survival on welfare with an emphasis on medicaid and the food stamp program. *Journal of Public Policy and Marketing, 15*(1), 118–127.

Horn, N. (1994). *Cultivating Customers: Market Women in Harare, Zimbabwe*. Boulder, CO: Lynne Reiner.

Itzin, C. and Phillipson, C. (1993). *Age barriers at work: Maximising the potential of mature and older workers*. Solihull, England: Metropolitan Authorities Recruitment Agency.

Jovičić, M. and Milojević, T. (August 2010). *Poverty and inequality changes in Serbia as the result of global instability*. Presented at The 11th bi-annual Conference of the EACES, Tartu, Estonia.

Lazear, E. (1995). *Personnel Economics*. Cambridge, UK: MIT Press.

Loretto, W., Duncan, C. and White, P. (2000). Ageism and employment: Controversies, ambiguities and younger people's perceptions. *Ageing and Society 20*(3), 279–302.

MacNicol, J. (2006). *Age Discrimination: A Historical and Contemporary Analysis*. Cambridge, UK: Cambridge University Press.

Milanovic, B. (1998), *Explaining the increase in inequality during transition* (Policy, Research Working Paper Series No. 1935). Washington DC: The World Bank.

Ngo, H.Y., Tang, C. and Au, W. (2002). Behavioural responses to employment discrimination: A study of Hong Kong workers. *International Journal of Human Resource Management, 13*(8), 1206–1223.

Onyx, J. (1998). Older women workers: A double jeopardy? In M. Patrickson and L. Hartmann (Eds), *Managing an Ageing Workforce* (pp. 88–105). Warriewood, NSW: Business and Professional Publishing.

Radović-Marković, M. (2007). *The Perspective of Women's Entrepreneurship in the Age of Globalization*. Charlotte, NC: IAP.

Radović-Marković, M. (2009). Globalization and gender participation in the informal sector in developing and transitional countries. *E+M Economics and Management Journal, 4*, 6–16.

Radović-Marković, M. (2011). Critical employment analysis: Theory, methodology and research. *Journal of Security and Sustainability Issues, 1*(2), 113–121. Retrieved April 2012 from www.lka.lt/index.php/lt/217049/.

Reinharz, S. (1986). Friends or foes: Gerontological and feminist theory. *Women's Studies International Forum, 9*(5), 503–514.

Riach, P.A. and Rich, J. (2002). Field experiments of discrimination in the market place. *The Economic Journal, 112*(483), F480–F518.

Riger, S. and Galligan, P. (1980). Women in management: An exploration of competing paradigms. *American Psychologist, 35*(10), 902–910.

Robertson, C. (1998). Women Entrepreneurs? Trade and the gender division of labor in Nairobi. In A. Spring and B. McDade (Eds), *African Entrepreneurship: Theory and Reality* (pp. 109–127). Gainesville, FL: University Press of Florida.

Roos, D. and Gladwin, C. (2000). Patriarchal gender ideologies and changes in women's commercial production in Cameroon. In A. Spring (Ed.), *Women Farmers and Commercial Ventures: Increasing Food Security in Developing Countries* (pp. 41–64). Boulder, CO: Lynne Rienner.

Rutkowski, J. (1996). *Changes in the wage structure during economic transition in central and Eastern Europe* (Technical Paper No 340). Washington DC: The World Bank Group.

Spariosu, T. (2007). Hidden economy in OECD and transition countries. In *Gender and Informal Economy in Developing, Developed and Transition Countries* (pp. 89–98). Lagos, Nigeria: ICEA and Prentice Consult.

United Nations (2002). *Report of the Second World Assembly on Ageing, Madrid, 8–12 April 2002* (A/CONF.197/9). New York: United Nations.

Warr, P. (1994). Age and job performance. In S. Jan and R. Cremer (Eds), *Work and Aging: A European Perspective* (pp. 309–322). London: Taylor and Francis.

Wilson, C. (2006). The price of age discrimination: When older workers face discrimination, everybody loses. *Gallup Management Journal, 6*(6). http://gmj.gallup.com/content/23164/price-age-discrimination.aspx.

7

Women in Managerial Jobs

Introduction

Typically, males have been known to dominate management positions, despite women having become more educated and career-oriented over the years. Although negative attitudes regarding women's qualifications for and performance in management persist, strong gains have been made by women in management and in acceptance of how their management styles differ. In this line, researchers are particularly interested in whether a management style that is typically associated with women – defined as more nurturing and less authoritarian – will become a more popular management style as the workplace shifts to a more team-oriented atmosphere that thrives on a less "directive" approach. In larger companies, men gain operations experience earlier in their careers, which qualifies them for the top jobs. Research shows, however, that men and women are equally effective. As decision makers learn that women are able to manage equally as effective as men, it is hoped that they will give women greater responsibilities. However when there is a bias against women as managers their access to higher positions is restricted, and so they are not given the chance to demonstrate their abilities for responsibility.

The Management Position of Women through History

Historically, women have been underrepresented in management positions (Carter and Silva, 2010). In the 1970s, women comprised only 19 per cent of all management positions in the United States, with similar findings around the globe (Schein, 2007). Studies conducted at that time revealed much of this problem could be attributed to stereotyping the traits needed in management and traits that men possess and women do not (Schein, 2007). Leadership, the desire for responsibility and objectivity are all traits attributed to managers as well as men; women were perceived as not possessing these traits

(Schein, 2007). This led to the attitude of "think manager–think male" that was sustained throughout much of the 1970s (Schein, 2007).

Since the 1970s, progress has been made in increasing management positions held by women, although women currently only make up 3 per cent of Fortune 500 CEOs and less than 15 per cent of corporate executives worldwide (Carter and Silva, 2010). Several reasons exist for such a persistent underrepresentation of women in management. The simplest of all these explanations is that the "think manager–think male" gender stereotyping is still prevalent in society (Schein, 2007). Male executives and male business students continue to perceive males as having more managerial traits, while perceiving that females lack the necessary traits (Schein, 2007). Similar studies conducted in Germany, the UK, China and Japan all reveal gender stereotyping among male and female business students; female students in the United States did not gender stereotype managerial positions (Schein, 2007).

This persistent gender stereotyping is sometimes referred to as the person-centred view of why women do not hold management positions (Crampton and Mishra, 1999). The person-centred view states that women do not hold management positions due to certain traits they do or do not possess (Crampton and Mishra, 1999, p. 89). In addition, while women perceive gender stereotyping as a barrier to career advancement, male CEOs and executives do not see gender stereotyping as a problem; rather they see a lack of experience as a hindrance to women's managerial advancement (Schein, 2007).

Cultural influences have also influenced women in management. There are still widely-held beliefs that women do not have aspirations to become managers and instead prefer to focus on having a family (Crampton and Mishra, 1999). Child care responsibilities as well as household chores are still largely considered women's work (Crampton and Mishra, 1999). Maternity leave has also been described by some women as detrimental to their career path, causing a loss of momentum and fear that they have lost their place within an organization (Crampton and Mishra, 1999).

The improved position of woman has enormous social implications, but women still only hold less than one of 20 top management positions in high-profile Fortune 500 corporations – only a slight increase over the past 20 years (Catalyst, 2009). Part of the reason is that, as people move up in leadership positions, the pyramid narrows to contain fewer individuals.

According to the US Bureau of Labor Statistics, nearly one in four chief executives is now a woman (Catalyst, 2009). Statistics from 1995 to 2009 show that the number of women among the Fortune 500 CEOs has gradually increased (Catalyst, 2009).

Women versus Men Managers

Despite both men and women being capable of being good managers, there are still differences in the leadership of men and women managers. Research has shown that women tend to focus more on interpersonal relationships, involving employees in decision making, and monitoring feedback from employees (Melero, 2010). Women tend to focus more on people-management practices, displaying individualized attention to employees more frequently than men (Melero, 2010). Women managers sometimes describe their leadership style as transformational, meaning that; workers transform their own self-interest into goals that will serve the greater good of the organization (Crampton and Mishra, 1999). In contrast, men are considered more transactional, that is, managing through various transactions between themselves and subordinates; a system of rewards and punishments (Crampton and Mishra, 1999). Women have typically been viewed as better suited for participatory management styles, due to better use of communication and public relations skills (Crampton and Mishra, 1999). In sum, most of the information available describes women and men as having different management styles, with one not being better than the other (Melero, 2010).

Since research shows that men and women have differing management styles, *Men's Health* magazine (2009) published some helpful tips from experienced female sources as guidelines for men interacting with female bosses:

- Women are more comfortable with cooperation than with hot-dogging. "Women are much more into networks of connections and involvement," says Karen Lawson, president of her own management-consulting firm in Philadelphia. "They want input, and they're often interpreted by men as being indecisive, when that's not it at all. They're just being consultative" (*Men's Health*, 2009).

- The boss may nod when you speak, but it doesn't mean she's agreeing to what you're saying. "She's indicating, 'Yes, I'm listening,' and encouraging you to go on, but it's not to be interpreted as agreement," Lawson says. "She'll listen more and talk less in the boardroom, but don't take advantage of her silence," because she's simply taking account of opinions and "weighing all options before verbalizing her own opinion".

- If she talks about what happened on the golf course last weekend, don't think she's dropping hints. "Women often draw on personal experiences to illustrate a point or explain an idea," says Lawson.

- Be careful about how you oppose her. "Women tend to get defensive when challenged because they see it as a personal attack on their credibility," says Lawson, "whereas men see challenging as a sign of respect and equal treatment."

- When she says, "I'm sorry" it's not necessarily an apology for wrongdoing – she just may be showing that she understands. "Women tend to say, 'I'm sorry,' to express empathy or shared feeling, and men often interpret it incorrectly," Lawson says.

- If the boss comes to you and presents a problem that needs solving, don't dole out advice until she finishes.

- She's not necessarily a stickler for protocol. "Women will ask for team and individual input, with relationships and impact sometimes more important than rules," says Marilyn – president of The Consulting Team, in Mountain View, California. In addition, she concluded: "A man prefers to decide who's right and wrong, winner or loser, as in all sports games."

Barriers to Female Progress

Simply identifying the barriers that women face to gaining management positions does not solve the problem. Women, as well as men, must become familiar with these barriers, perceived or real, and learn ways to overcome them. Legal pressure and legislative action has been implemented over the past several decades to protect women from discrimination. In the United States, the Equal Pay Act, Title VII of the Civil Rights Act, Pregnancy Discrimination Act, and the Family and Medical Leave Act were all passed in order to protect women from discrimination, granting equal pay and securing jobs in the event of pregnancy (Jones and George, 2006). Although these equal employment opportunity laws can protect against discrimination, they don't necessarily change attitudes and beliefs regarding gender stereotyping. Legal pressures can encourage organizations, however, to examine the roles of women in their organization and make decisions accordingly (Schein, 2007).

Recently, discrimination practices have been brought to light due to a lawsuit brought about by six female employees of Wal-Mart (Jones and George, 2006). This class-action lawsuit alleges women are purposely placed in low-level positions, while given no chance for advancement (Jones and George, 2006). Within Wal-Mart, 72 per cent of employees are female, but only 33 per cent of managers are female (Jones and George, 2006). Recently, the case was presented to the US Supreme Court. In a victory for Wal-Mart, the Court ruled that the case was too broad for class-action status and that proof of discrimination must be provided in the form of company policy rather than in statistics alone. In discussing the evidence in the case, Savage (2011) stated: "The plaintiffs' evidence, including class members' tales of their own experience, suggests that gender bias suffused Wal-Mart's company culture."

In addition to legal protections implemented by the Government, individual employees in the US can also take actions to advance their careers and break through the glass ceiling. Having a clearly defined career path with specific objectives and goals in mind, as well as being aware of the time, dedication and hard work needed to meet those goals, can help female employees have a successful career (Crampton and Mishra, 1999). Competition is often fierce for positions in management and women must learn to be confident, assertive and determined (Crampton and Mishra, 1999).

Delegation is a large part of management, and women must learn to analyse the task to be completed, decide what aspect can be delegated and how it can be delegated, choose the appropriate employee, delegate the task and follow-up to ensure that it is completed (Crampton and Mishra, 1999). Gaining respect and utilizing their power, the organization can help women exercise their management role, as well as to navigate organizational politics (Crampton and Mishra, 1999).

Creating a Supportive Business Environment for Women

Fostering an environment that is conducive to women's lives can help balance work and home life for many managers (Radović-Marković, 2012). Flexible schedules, job sharing among part-time employees, compressed work weeks, childcare leave and pregnancy leave can help balance work and family responsibilities (Crampton and Mishra, 1999). Training, education and career development opportunities must be afforded to both men and women, and organizations should be an institution that can provide opportunities (Crampton and Mishra, 1999). In this context, organizations can develop programmes and policies to combat barriers and promote gender equity. If an organization finds it is not placing employees in the positions they are most qualified for, particularly women, a change is necessary following an evaluation of how practices can be improved. Such a change will be beneficial for the individuals involved as well as for the society at large. It has been suggested that role models and mentors, who serve as teachers, sponsors, devil's advocates and coaches, can influence aspiring female managers (Crampton and Mishra, 1999).

Some research has shown that women are greatly influenced by their first managers (Carter and Silva, 2010). Having a difficult manager was cited by almost a quarter of female respondents when asked why they left their first job. Having a supportive and mentoring manager is important for employee retention and for allowing individuals to climb up the corporate ladder within an organization (Carter and Silva, 2010).

When businesses provide such opportunities, happier families result from the increased work and family balance introduced by women managers. Reduced turnover and reduced absenteeism are positively correlated with policies that take family and personal life into account, such as flexible scheduling, child and elder care, and special needs assistance (Tarr-Whelan, 2009). These results contribute to greater stability and profits for the organization, meaning more overall success. Perhaps the implementation of such policies signals the type of emotional intelligence women possess that men score lower on: interpersonal skills, social responsibility and awareness of emotions, as opposed to men's greater intrapersonal skills, ability to cope well with stress, higher self-regard, and greater optimism (Condren et al., 2006). Although Emotional Quotient Inventory (EQ-i) is considered a "soft skill" it has been identified to significantly improve workplace efficiency for managers, leaders and employees (Connell et. al., 2002). And, although men also possess certain types of emotional intelligence, the new global marketplace requires increased consideration of diversity and, with it, self-awareness.

Women's contribution has never been more important, as evidenced by Anne Levine. She is an owner of Applied Building Technologies, a company based in Baltimore, MD specializing in heating, ventilation and air conditioning (HVAC) and exhaust cleaning and building management, and has faced her own difficulties being a female entrepreneur and business owner. "Owning a company in a male-dominated field, gaining the respect of engineers and building managers has been vitally important and sometimes a daunting task" she concluded.

Conclusions

We can conclude that men and women have different management styles in organizations. Women are still the minority in terms of leadership, and thus, there is pressure to give way to male-oriented organizational cultures. Regardless, men and women both have their associated talents and contributions in diverse circumstances. And stereotypes may not always apply, since some individuals are gender-atypical in their personalities and styles. However, research continues to find that women's management style has a few common elements: democratic, cooperative, inclusive, accepting of difference, interest in long-term benefit for all members, and more egalitarian than hierarchical or authoritarian.

These elements make for an environment suited to innovation, efficiency and progress, especially considering the demands of the changing world marketplace. In the meantime, experts suggest that both men and women learn to communicate with one another so that they may work together at their best with little confusion. They must learn each other's gender language, so to speak, and value the contributions each has to offer, while considering what is best for the success of their organization. Mentors can offer an excellent opportunity for employees to learn corporate culture first-hand in order to adopt desirable behaviours and attitudes (Crampton and Mishra, 1999).

Finally, we can point out that great strides have been made in advancing management roles for women. Despite these strides, women still lag behind men in the management field. Understanding the barriers that women face and implementing solutions to overcome them is vital in the corporate world. Changing perceptions will take some time, but continued discussion and analysis of the issue can help transform long-held beliefs and attitudes.

References

Carter, N.M. and Silva, C. (2010). Women in management: Delusions of progress. *Harvard Business Review, 88*(3), 19–21.

Catalyst Census of the Fortune 500 Reveals Women Missing From Critical Business Leadership. (December 2009). *Catalyst in the News*. Retrieved August 2011 from http://www.catalyst.org/press-release/161/2009-catalyst-census-of-the-fortune-500-reveals-women-missing-from-critical-business-leadership.

Condren, T., Hutchinson, S. and Martin, B. (2006). What does emotional intelligence and gender have to do with leadership effectiveness … Or does it? *Advancing Women in Leadership Online Journal, 21*. Retrieved 23 November 2006 from http://www.advancingwomen.com/awl/summer2006/Condren_Martin_Hutchinson.html.

Connell, J., Cross, B. and Parry, K. (2002). Leadership in the 21st century: Where is it leading us? *International Journal of Organisational Behaviour, 5*(2), 139–149. Retrieved 24 April 2010 from http:/209.85.129.132/search?q=cache:Ynh8ySqW7EJ:www.usq.edu.au/extrafiles/business/journals/HRMJournal/InternationalArticles/ConnellCrossParry2.pdf+personality+of+women+leaders+and+their+organization+behaviour&cd=10&hl=sr&ct=clnk.

Crampton, S.M. and Mishra, J.M. (1999). Women in management. *Public Personnel Management, 28*(1), 87–106.

Jones, G.R. and George, J.M. (2006). *Contemporary Management* (4th edn). New York, NY: McGraw Hill/Irwin.

Melero, E. (2010). Are workplaces with many women in management run differently? *Journal of Business Research, 64*(4), 385–393.

Men's Health (2009). Seven secrets to working for a woman. Retrieved May 2010 from http://www.menshealth.com/men/sex-relationships/decode-her/gender-and-work-how-to-handle-having-a-woman-boss/article/da3a99edbbbd201099edbbbd2010cfe793cd.

Radović-Marković, M. (2012). *Impact of Globalization on Organizational Culture, Behaviour and Gender Role*. Charlotte, NC: IAP.

Savage, D.G. (21 June 2011). Supreme Court blocks huge class-action suit against Wal-Mart. *Los Angeles Times*. Retrieved January 2012 from http://articles.latimes.com/2011/jun/21/nation/la-na-court-walmart-20110621.

Schein, V.E. (2007). Women in management: Reflections and projections. *Women in Management Review, 22*(1), 6–18.

Tarr-Whelan, L. (2009). *Women Lead the Way: Your Guide to Stepping up to Leadership and Changing the World*. San Francisco, CA: Berrett-Koehler.

PART II

Special Topics on Entrepreneurship

Introduction

In the second part of this book we explore different types of business opportunities. These sorts of opportunities, together with knowledge and technology give women choices, empowerment and enable them to be entrepreneurs. We focus here on rural entrepreneurship, home business and e-business. Fostering women by promoting rural women's entrepreneurship, home business and e-business is of key importance to alleviating poverty, driving innovation and to sustainable development. These opportunities offer a number of particular advantages for women entrepreneurs, such as flexible working hours, location at or near women's homes, and better work–life balance. Running these kinds of businesses increases women's self-confidence, improves their negotiating position within the household, and better involves them in decision-making processes. Nonetheless, as the first part of the book has indicated, female entrepreneurs also face particular obstacles and challenges when starting and expanding their businesses. The topics in this part of the book, whilst especially relevant to female empowerment and to overcoming those obstacles and challenges, are also of interest in relation to entrepreneurial activity more generally.

8

Rural Entrepreneurship

Introduction

Rural development is linked to entrepreneurship to a greater extent than ever before. Institutions and individuals promoting rural development now see entrepreneurship as a strategic development intervention that can accelerate the rural development process. Rural entrepreneurship has, in recent years, increasingly taken the leading role in the development of rural regions. This is due to a number of factors. In the first place, traditional economic activities based on routine agricultural production and those based on the use of natural resources struggle to survive and be competitive in the global market. In order to achieve agricultural development strategy must change. It is for this reason that experts in this field seek new sources that would help increase competitiveness.

Hence most researchers introduce new concepts and possibilities that can be implemented to create a new and sustainable economic development in rural regions. This development can be defined as "sustaining wealth and improving the production competencies of rural local communities or a long-term building of a stimulating environment that will foster these competencies" (Fieldsend and Nagy, 2006).

The new approach that has been developed during the last decade is linked to "bottom-up" rural development. This approach is based on the importance of the development of a community aided by local entrepreneurial initiatives and a clearly set goal to ensure a balanced technological development of rural regions. This balanced technological development of rural regions is meant to offer better employment opportunities and a higher quality of living. Namely, it permits opportunities for the agricultural regions to develop equally as fast as urban regions.

Rural Entrepreneurship, Concept and Definition

Rural entrepreneurship is a recent research area in the study of entrepreneurship. In recent years it has gained in importance as the prevailing method of fostering rural development. Important as it is, rural entrepreneurship has, nonetheless, only recently been clearly defined. In this domain, however, there is no universal definition, nor a universal concept of the study of rural entrepreneurship. Thus we attempted to formulate our own definition of rural entrepreneurship that would be all-comprehensive, both in its essence and in the aspects it covers. Accordingly, we define rural entrepreneurship as the creation of entrepreneurial associations that will ensure crucial economic, social and other changes in rural regions and improve these regions (Radović-Marković, 2009). This also includes the promotion of rural entrepreneurship by the governments devising a rural development policy based on investing in rural entrepreneurship. I will also focus my attention upon the causes of low profitability of agriculture in developing countries and in many transition countries, including Serbia. A majority of these countries are characterized by obsolete technology, poor training of the labour force in rural regions, and so on.

Hence rural entrepreneurship emerges in economically and socially backward regions, those with inadequate infrastructure, low level of education, unskilled work force and low incomes, where the level of local culture does not support it (Kulavczuk, 1998).

Since rural development policy has to observe local, regional and national aspects and potentials, it is not possible to formulate the best model of rural entrepreneurship development that would have a universal meaning and implementation.

The earliest and the most important concept of entrepreneurial activity in the agricultural sector is "production", as it was important to produce enough food to feed the members of the community. This concept prevailed in the 1950s and 1960s. In time, however, it became evident that this production concept cannot be the only one, so it was broadened by introducing the "price concept" into agricultural development policy. The farmers' responsibilities were thus a constrained concept that was promptly replaced by another with the aim of increasing their accountability. It was then that the concept of "cost structure optimization in the organization" was introduced.

This concept, however, was not aimed at future business challenges, nor did it observe the changes in the external business environment. In the 1990s it was replaced by a new concept, based on the "rural entrepreneurs' creativity and flexibility". The core idea of this concept was to provide new solutions to problems as well as new products. The trend was to develop small markets, be oriented to certain target groups and use new methods in solving problems.

Development of Rural Entrepreneurship in Developing Countries

The interest in rural entrepreneurship research has increased in the past few years in the European Union (EU) countries as a result of numerous programmes for entrepreneurship in remote rural areas. Namely, the countries that have only recently joined the EU expressed their need for a deeper comprehension of rural entrepreneurship processes in the economies in transition (Radović-Marković, 2009).

Despite an increased interest among the new member states of the EU, the current literatures in this field generally focus on the developed countries. Some of this research shows that small and medium-sized enterprises (SMEs) in rural regions make up 28 per cent to 30 per cent of the total number of all businesses in the developed countries such as Canada and the United States.

Regardless of the high share held by SMEs, a large number of rural entrepreneurs encounter serious problems, such as remoteness of markets, high shipping and other costs, problems in recruiting qualified labour force, and low profit rates compared to firms in urban regions. The comparison of entrepreneurs in urban and in rural regions is presented in Table 8.1.

On the basis of these figures, we can conclude that the number of women business owners in rural areas is smaller than in the urban areas of Canada. Also, the number of rural entrepreneurs who join the businesses of their close relatives is considerably higher than the number of such entrepreneurs in urban areas.

About 1.5 billion people, that is, nearly 60 per cent of the developing countries' workforce, are engaged in agriculture and agricultural productivity. Despite women's position having gradually improved in developing countries, they remain far behind women in developed countries in terms of: their

Table 8.1   Entrepreneur profile in rural and urban areas in Canada, 2004

Entrepreneurs in rural areas	Characteristics	Entrepreneurs in urban areas
12% of businesses are in women and 46% are in men ownership	Gender	16% of businesses are in women and 55% are in men ownership
81% have more than 10 years of managerial experience	Managerial experience	65% have more than 10 years of managerial experience
6% of enterprises earn income from exports	Export activity	9% of enterprises earn income from exports
64% are beginners in business, while 22 % join the businesses of their close relatives	Manner in which the business is started	80% are beginners in business, while 5% join the businesses of their close relatives

Source: SME Financing Data Initiative (2004). *Statistics Canada, Survey on Financing of Small and Medium Enterprises, 2004.*

educational level, working in jobs that pay less or not at all, working under difficult conditions, the absence of suitable public and private financing, lack of role models in entrepreneurship, lack of relevant networks, women's mobility and so forth.

In this context, the following important guidelines must be followed in the development of rural entrepreneurship:

- fostering the setting up of businesses, but also motivating entrepreneurs to continually improve them;

- networking of entrepreneurs in order to define the areas that can bring highest profits, which should help the planning and orientation of business activities;

- entrepreneurs should make decisions in favour of both their own business and their environment;

- entrepreneurs should pay attention to environmental protection when creating entrepreneur activities;

- provision of a better future for rural families and reducing the migration of young people into cities;

- State institutions must appreciate the value of rural entrepreneurship and incorporate it into the economic strategy of the country's development, and support its development. They must also help individual entrepreneurs formalize their activities, thus contributing to their local communities by paying taxes. Special programmes should be devised to help and support women, young workers, old persons and the self-employed to ensure their social inclusion.

The development of rural entrepreneurship in this manner would bring major benefits, not only to the local community but to the entire society in several of its domains, such as:

- a larger number of entrepreneurs – an increased number of new businesses;

- more competent entrepreneurs – entrepreneurs who have the knowledge and skills needed in their businesses;

- growth and expansion of businesses – businesses boost production and sales, as well as create new jobs that absorb the local labour force;

- economic benefits for the local community – by way of tax payments.

In many developing countries, enterprise development centres have been successful at assisting the development of start-up enterprises. Such efforts should help women obtain necessary training and support to start businesses for food production, conservation and marketing as well as establish themselves a village leaders who are engaged in the community's development and in the design and implementation of activities to improve their livelihoods (Radović-Marković, 2010).

In our opinion, training programmes should be available not only to women with low income and who are affected by climate hazards, but also to their instructors and teachers. The teachers have to complete the training to meet and share experiences, support and encourage one another, and generate ideas and solutions.

The Case of African Women Farmers

Women in Africa work in agriculture and in food production and, much less, in non-agricultural activities. Namely, in Africa, women farmers produce up to 90 per cent of the continent's food, according to the UN Food and Agriculture Organization (FAO), hence it is they who are most affected by climate changes (Radović-Marković, 2010).They are most at risk of climate change because they are more dependent on agriculture and water resource changes than men because of their low socio-economic and legal status. Climate change hits their agricultural productivity through floods, pests and catastrophic events, as well as through temperature changes.

Although women are responsible for growing up to 90 per cent of food in Africa, it is estimated they own only about 1 per cent of the land. Women workers in Africa also tend to be concentrated in a narrower range of "female" activities in tasks that require less or no skills and are paid less than men. In Africa, women work almost as unpaid family workers in agriculture with low technology and primitive farming practices. Their share of informal sector employment has remained high in Africa (60–80 per cent), diminishing their capabilities to participate in decision making. In addition, women in rural areas lack knowledge about environment disasters, information and instruments to collect data, financial resources to combat climate change, and sufficient involvement in social strategies on climate change risks. In other words, the lack of gender equality in Africa has limited the contribution of women to the management of hazards in their adaptation to climate change. Empowering women is necessary by bringing them into the mainstream of development and by improving their economic status and providing them with new opportunities for income generation, self-employment and entrepreneurship in different socio-economic sectors.

A new approach and consideration of hidden opportunities for women should be created for the purpose of meeting business and environmental challenges.

Conclusions

The environmental and rural issues should not to be considered separately from economy and entrepreneurship. Successful agricultural business involves innovations that should support women and marginalized groups to improve their lives and to reduce food shortage as well as to improve their health. Namely, agriculture can produce food while protecting soils, water and biodiversity. It creates new jobs and opens new employment opportunities and at the same time keeps our planet clean. Therefore, for many rural women, entrepreneurship is part of a broader livelihood strategy, often undertaken on a part-time basis, and where it is difficult to separate production and reproduction tasks, as well as market and non-market work (International Labour Organization, 2001). In developing countries women work almost as unpaid family workers in agriculture with low technology and primitive farming practices.

Rural entrepreneurship has an enormous employment potential. Women see it as an employment opportunity near their homes that provides independence and reduces the need for social support. Farmers see it as an instrument for improving farm earnings and achieving a better standard of living. However, the acceptance of entrepreneurship as a central development force by itself will not result in rural development and the progress of rural enterprises. It must be pointed out that the creation of such an environment begins at the national level with the foundation of policies for macro-economic stability.

We also discussed what local communities can do to foster rural entrepreneurship in general. In line with this, we especially stressed that creating small businesses in rural areas is of great importance for the restructuring and modernization of the rural regions/villages and for improving the living conditions there. In addition, it includes creating State policies with programmes to aid the development of entrepreneurship. An efficient concept of rural entrepreneurship has to focus on the transformation of the local business culture to be adopted by the local rural population as their own career choice. Such a transformation cannot be achieved through the implementation of State programmes alone.

These concepts should also be studied at schools, among young people who should acquire education in entrepreneurship while they are still very young.

References

Fieldsend, A. and Nagy, J. (2006). Constraints on rural entrepreneurship in eastern Hungary. *Proceedings from the First International Conference on Agriculture and Rural Development*. Topusko, Croatia, 23–25 November.

International Labour Organization, Mayoux, L. (2001). *Jobs, gender and small enterprises: getting the policy environment right.* SEED Working Paper No. 15. Geneva.

Kulawczuk, P. (1998). The development of entrepreneurship in rural areas. In J.D. Kimball (Ed.), *The Transfer of Power: Decentralization in Central and Eastern Europe* (pp. 97–109). Budapest, Hungary: The Local Government and Public Service Reform Initiative.

Radović-Marković, M. (2009). *Types of Entrepreneurship.* Belgrade, Serbia: IES.

Radović-Marković, M. (2010). Importance of female entrepreneurship in tackling climate change. In *Women's Leadership in Energy and Climate Change.* Symposium conducted at the meeting of Said Business School, 16 June, Oxford, Great Britain.

SME Financing Data Initiative (2004). *Statistics Canada, Survey on Financing of Small and Medium Enterprises, 2004* [Data]. Retrieved May 2007 http://www.sme-fdi.gc.ca/eic/site/sme_fdi-prf_pme.nsf/eng/01561.html.

9

Virtual Entrepreneurship

Definition of Virtual Organizations

Information systems play a vital role in e-business and e-commerce operations, enterprise collaboration and management, and in the strategic success of businesses that must operate in an Internet-worked global environment. The Internet services, in conjunction with the more widely-used communication media, provide the broadest enhancement of information and communication resources (Radović-Marković, 2011).

> Virtual organization is a temporary network of independent business units – suppliers, customers, and even rivals – linked by information and communication technology to share skills, costs and access to different markets. This organizational model is flexible – groups of collaborators quickly unite to exploit a specific opportunity. In its most elementary form, the concept depicts any organization that interacts with other organizations to create a virtual corporation and that only contributes within the scope of its core competency. Central in the development of virtual organization is technology. Teams of people in different companies work together, via a computer network in real time. (Byrne, 1993)

This definition provides a clear structural perspective and a detailed picture of what makes a virtual organization.

Characteristics of Virtual Organizations

Virtual organizations are characterized by: (a) highly dynamic processes; (b) contractual relationships among entities; (c) edgeless, permeable boundaries; and (d) reconfigurable structures (DeSanctis and Monge, 1998).

As the virtual organization consists of a network of independent companies, each of these companies contributes with its core competency. The organization that initiates the cooperation defines the most appropriate business processes, which in turn are complementary to the business skills of different firms. The synergy effect that is the result of combining all the core competencies allows for creating an organization that meets the customer requirements in a flexible manner. According to Aken et al. (1998), a virtual organization has to have its own identity. If the identity of a partner remains visible alongside the identity of the organization, it is defined as a "loosely coupled virtual organization" whereas a "tightly coupled virtual organization" appears to customers as a joint organization. The development of information and communication technologies solved the differences in distances between virtual organizations so they can work together.

The partners in the virtual organization are equal; hence it is an organization without hierarchy. A favourable effect of such an architecture results in an improved organizational efficiency and responsibility (Bultje and Van, 1998).

The organizations consist of a network of autonomous companies, hence such architecture is also known as network architecture. It differs from a hierarchical architecture by the large number of lateral communications that make this organizational structure highly coordination-intensive.

There are different virtual organization networking modalities, depending on the degree of collaboration and management required, and hence different types of information to be shared. The types of information needed to be shared to manage a virtual organization on an e-level are the following:

- Planning (P): information used to define a common purpose, to determine the scope and orientation of work of the entire virtual organization.

- Operational (O): information on the activities to be performed on a daily basis for each member.

- Coordinating (C): information flows to ensure that operational activities achieve their goal effectively.

Virtual Culture as a Basis for Effective Communication in Virtual Organizations

An organization that has a large proportion of employees working in the virtual workplace faces distinct challenges related to building an organizational culture. When building a culture within a virtual firm, managers have numerous tools at their disposal to compensate for the lack of social context, geographical location and the normal behaviours of a non-virtual firm. Managers of a virtual firm need to focus on results since they may not be able to see all of the work that is being done. They also need to be able to delegate and keep track of projects and work. Managers of a virtual firm should not be micro-managers, as this style will most likely not be effective.

Another requirement for a manager in a virtual organization is that he or she needs to be able to motivate his or her employees to go online. Since the majority of the firm's work will be online, it is important for the employees to be able to access the information they need to do their jobs. This can be done by putting important news and updated online matter in a place where the employees will also find other job-related information. If the majority of the firm's work will be online, it is important to have an easy-to-use system. Employees will not want to go online or use systems that are difficult to use and take too much time. When building a system, it is important to get opinions from the people who will be using it. In addition, with all of the tools and systems that will be in place for a virtual firm, it is important that the employees know when and how to use the tools and systems they have access to. Sometimes it makes better business sense to meet a person face-to-face that try to communicate via e-mail. This needs to be understood by everyone, especially when dealing with clients.

Managers also need to be able to communicate through multiple channels on both formal and informal levels. There are a number of features of a virtual firm that should be considered as part of the culture to successfully run and manage the firm. The first feature of the culture of a virtual firm is trust (Van de Bunt-Kokhuis, 2000). Since a manager cannot always see his or her employees, they must be able to trust that their employees are doing the work that they are supposed to be doing. It should also be noted that since the majority of work will be done online, most of this work can be easily monitored and employees may worry about being spied on.

The second feature of the culture of a virtual firm is leadership. It is important that a company's leaders show the behaviour that they want their employees to exhibit. These are the role models of the firm that will set the tone for the entire company.

The third feature is that a virtual company needs to be comfortable with being different and doing things differently. Virtual companies will always be different from traditional companies, and the culture needs to reflect that. In addition, the employees must be able to work in an environment that may not be what they are accustomed to.

The fourth feature of a virtual company is that there will be some positions within the company that do very boring work, for example, those in a call centre or at a help desk (Van de Bunt-Kokhuis, 2000). These employees will most likely be low paid, so rewards and incentives need to be considered to reduce the turnover and increase efficiency.

The fifth feature of a virtual company is the emphasis on communication. All the employees of a virtual company need to have good communication skills, including upper-level management. In a virtual company, employees do not have the ability to stop by a co-worker's office to quickly discuss a project. Instead, they will need to pick up the phone or send an e-mail, neither of which has the same effect as a face-to-face meeting. It is also difficult to show emotions in an e-mail, and sometimes over the phone. Because of this, employees need to learn to express themselves and to listen effectively. This includes discussions during group meetings or when working on team projects.

The sixth feature of a virtual company is the need for good communication within the company. Since employees do not see each other regularly as in a traditional company, it is important to establish a connectedness of employees. This will make the company have more of a family feel and will improve motivation.

The seventh feature is shared values. In order to have a successful virtual company everyone involved needs to share the same values. This is even more important in a virtual company because the company's values cannot be instilled on a daily basis as in the traditional company due to the lack of physical connection.

The eighth feature is that virtual companies will have slightly different jobs than those in the traditional companies. For example, a traditional secretary may be replaced by a virtual assistant.

Communication in Virtual Organizations

Communication plays a key role in the work of virtual organizations. Without communication, the boundaries of operations of a virtual entity would be impossible to determine at any level (DeSanctis and Monge, 1998).

In surveying these four areas, it is important to bear in mind that a majority of findings were obtained on the basis of the study of electronic mail and e-conferencing; other forms of electronic communication, such as group voting, documentation management systems or electronic data exchange are not included. Furthermore, a large amount of research compares the modalities of electronic communication with oral speech, especially with direct, face-to-face communication, despite the fact that electronic communications display a large number of properties similar to the written form of communication. Like face-to-face communication, electronic communication is interactive. The result is that the behaviour in electronic communication takes on the characteristics of both written documents and informal speech (Wilkins, 1991).

For the communication to be successful, it is necessary that communicators have equal levels of knowledge, which is difficult to achieve without physical and linguistic presence. This means that the lack of face-to-face contact in electronic communication may have a negative impact upon understanding the message, but the literature is rather ambiguous on this issue. The research on understanding electronic communication has concluded that there are a number of difficulties in understanding the meaning of the information and managing the feedback during an exchange of information.

Regardless of the advantage in terms of the speed and distance of exchanges of information electronically, electronic communication revealed some additional misconceptions, for example, tasks will not be completed faster if done electronically. It has also been shown, however, that the lack of visualization has not significantly disturbed conversation and its ability to be understood in case of synchronous communication via discussion groups (Marshall and Novick, 1995). Visualization is necessary, however, in resolving certain conflicting situations and complex activities, as well as in overcoming certain social and cultural differences.

The inter-organizational communication among virtual organizations assumes that most communication is conducted through transaction exchange within the network, which allows for a faster and larger information flow, especially in task setting, whereas a smaller amount of information is related to hierarchal flows. The communication among the departments of equal rank within the organization is conducted via synchronous technologies.

In the case that more consensus among the participants on different levels is required, and in case non-synchronous communication is pursued, the result may be a highly intensive exchange of messages so that a more detailed harmonization and understanding can be achieved.

Conclusions

Communication is fundamental to any form of organization; however, it is especially important for virtual organizations. Compared to more traditional settings, communication processes in virtual contexts are expected to be rapid, customized, temporary, larger in volume, more formal and more relationship-based (DeSanctis and Monge, 1998).

While technology is an important aspect of a virtual firm, there is still a human component that serves for decision making and activities that require judgment. In these terms, there is definitely a shift in the structure of a virtual firm. For instance, there seems to be less middle management within a virtual firm than in a traditional firm.

Some firms have developed employee orientation tools to guide them through the virtual work. This may include written guidelines, training and networks for colleagues. Virtual firms should consider a computer-based chat room, where employees can work on projects with other team members and get information on the work they are doing. They should also have a social protocol for employees and teams that have information on common cultural values. In addition to e-mail, a virtual firm needs to have access to video and audio conferencing. This will permit employees and managers to work with one another from a distance and have the effect of working from the same location.

A virtual firm needs to be able to balance the virtual with the face-to-face. It should also make sure it can manage schedules online and require employees to be at work on time, even though they do not have to physically show up. In addition to attendance, it is important to make sure that employees participate in meetings and in work in a virtual setting. Many virtual firms are sharing corporate information and even financial information with their employees. This ensures a better relationship between the upper-level management and employees. In addition, there seems to be a more even division of power. This is linked directly to the virtual culture of empowerment and self-control.

A virtual company needs a technology infrastructure to survive, but there is also a need to have a solid cultural infrastructure in place that not only deals with the human aspect but with the technology aspect as well.

With the further development of new technologies, we expect that modalities of communication will continue to experience radical changes in virtual enterprises. It is not easy to predict the direction these changes will take, but what is certain is that they will depend not only on technological change but also on the change in employee awareness in virtual firms. In other words, they will depend on their ability to overcome the present differences (gender, language, emotional, cultural, perceptional and others) and create an efficient communication in virtual firms. Therefore, the human factor will play a role in improving communication in virtual firms as important as that of the development and improvement of the present technologies.

References

Aken, J. van, Hop, L. and Post, G.J.J. (1998). The virtual organization: A special mode of strong interorganizational cooperation. In M.A. Hitt, J.E. Ricart, I. Costa and R.D. Nixon (Eds), *Managing Strategically in an Interconnected World*, Chichester, UK: John Wiley and Sons.

Bultje, R. and Van, W.J. (1998). Taxonomy of virtual organisations, based on definitions, characteristics and typology. *VoNet: The Newsletter*, 2(3), 7–20.

Byrne, J.A. (1993). The virtual corporation, *Business Week*, 8 February, 98–102.

DeSanctis, G. and Fulk, J. (Eds) (1999). *Shaping Organization Form: Communication, Connection and Community*. Newbury Park, CA: Sage.

DeSanctis, G. and Monge, P. (1998). Communication processes for virtual organizations, *Journal of Computer-Mediated Communication*, 3(4), 693–703.

Marshall, C. and Novick, D. (1995). Conversational effectiveness and multimedia communications. *Information Technology and People*, 8(1), 54–79.

Radović-Marković, M. (2011). *Organizational Behaviour and Culture: Globalization and the Changing Environment of Organizations*. Saarbrücken, Germany: VDM Verlag Dr. Muller.

Van de Bunt-Kokhuis, S. (2000). The virtual workplace and the company culture employee oriented tools to build a corporate web culture. *Management site for and by professionals*. Retrieved May 2009 from http://www.managementsite. com/261/The-virtual-workplace-and-the-company-culture.aspx.

Wilkins, H. (1991). Computer talk: Long-distance conversations by computer. *Written Communication*, 8, 56–78.

10

Project-based Firms

Introduction

Project management comprises numerous economic activities that greatly contribute to the modern economy. The need for project management evolved from the need to coordinate work among sectors and professions, as well as from the facilities offered by the organized work on a project. Project management has in the past decade become vitally important for numerous firms and managers. Projects are the preferential vehicle to implement and manage change through two main lines of action: growing competitiveness in the range of supply and productivity improvement. Faced with this inevitable reality, most organizations around the globe spend over half of their annual budget in the execution of projects. In 2011 alone, the world spent one-fifth of its GDP (12 trillion US dollars) on projects (Project Management Institute, 2011).

Organizations are no longer places where managers and other employees are static and perform routine activities. Projects and project-based firms provide a rich context for studying different organizational phenomena and temporary organizations. The context is characterized by complex projects that are implemented in dynamic environments and consist of multiple firms in various roles, with each firm and project having its own business objectives (Kujala et al., 2012). In other words, every project is unique in some sense, hence it cannot be prepared and implemented routinely; new solutions have to be sought. It is also true that collaborators from many countries become engaged in projects, so project management achieves its global dimension.

Definition of Project Management

The history of "a project" as an academic term is not that old, but when we look back to the beginning of civilization, some of the actual achievements such as the Great Wall of China or the Pyramids in Egypt, would be called "projects" today (Shenhar and Dvir, 2007). In its modern form, project management was first devised and implemented in the 1960s, however, its roots can be traced further back, to the last decade of the nineteenth century (Radović-Marković, 2012). Project management has a defined beginning and end; it is not a continual process. It may occasionally require resources, contrary to organizations, which have resources that are permanently engaged.

Project management in literature is also frequently presented as a triangle, as its three most important factors are time, quality of activity and cost.

Project-based Organizations

Organizations in this category are also known as temporary organizations. Organizations initiate projects and participate in projects to improve innovative capacity, to carry out rapid changes, and to enhance adaptive capability (Whitley, 2006). Projects can be seen as a source of competitive advantage and they can serve as strategic arenas to develop new capabilities that can be reused in future business (Radović-Marković and Omolaja, 2011).

In business, project management offers an invaluable and highly effective structure within which to identify and focus on the priorities, track and measure performance, overcome challenges and issues, address unforeseen risks as they arise, and achieve higher performance and probability of success in each business endeavour. The behaviour, responsiveness and relationships that exist among such organizational members are not formalized, that is, they are not based on formal rules, regulations and procedures.

The degree of dynamism may also depend on the size of the projects. Industries like construction and engineering, with long project durations, will be less dynamic than IT or product development, with short project durations.

There are certain critical conditions that a good project-based organizational structure must satisfy. Also referred to as the main features or characteristics of the modern organization, these are as follows (Radović-Marković, 2007):

- Flexibility in Operations: Every organization should be flexible enough in such a way that unanticipated changes are accommodated. This would prevent the organization from suffering any form of adjustment lag.

- Consultation and Participation: This implies that every organizational structure must encourage (or allow room for) consultation and participation in decision-making processes among the organizational members.

- Purposive Activity: All efforts in the organization must be focused, directed or channelled toward the accomplishment of the predetermined individual, department and corporate goals.

- Delegation: This implies that operations and activities must be well assigned, appropriate authority must be delegated for their effective performance and adequate allowance must be provided as safeguards for management control.

- Differentiation: This implies that the staff structure, functions and responsibilities must be well differentiated, and techniques of inter-divisional communication clearly determined.

- Clear Lines of Communication: This means that there should be clear, short and direct lines of communication between an employee and his superior officer, who is responsible for the supervision of the work. In addition, there must be clear lines of authority and information among employees in the organization. This prevents conflict, friction and unnecessary rivalries among the staff.

- Strategy: The organization must approach its strategy, goals and work from the top down, and implement a direct alignment among all three.

Organizations that range from global businesses to governments have identified project management and skilled project managers as the key to their success. The basic functions of project management include the same functions that characterize other types of management, such as planning.

It comprises the selection of tasks to be accomplished in order to secure organizational goals, the manner in which they are to be accomplished and the time span in which they have to be completed. Planning is the most fundamental phase of the management process. It allows managers to run the firm in an appropriate direction and thus build the basis for other management functions.

Planning also makes it possible to identify the type of organizational structure required for a specific type of business, as well as to determine the qualification, gender and other structures of the employees required for a business, define the leadership style and the type of control required to accomplish the set tasks and goals. Planning is a dynamic process since every business is conducted in a changing environment.

When designing a project, the task of the project manager is to define the vision, which he does together with his team. The vision is defined as it would appear in the function of time, although still imaginary. They also have to explain what are their unbiased expectations regarding the realization of this vision. In other words, their task is to create and conceptualize an idea that contains the results of empirical research and analysis. This helps them reduce the prediction errors from the beginning and make the project more successful in its practical implementation.

Project managers also have to think strategically, looking ahead for what is needed and which business steps must be taken in the near or a relatively near future. They must not be narrow-minded: if the project, for example, focuses on the expansion of business, they have to have an a priori vision of the direction in which the firm should develop in the future. Namely, the key managerial task is the integration of project-based learning into the organization. In case of an existing project, managers must identify possible errors and flaws, employing their experience and regarding the development trends. Only thus will they be able to further develop and expand the business.

We would like to stress that the demand for project professionals is permanently increasing, with an average of 1.2 million projected new jobs to be filled each year for the next decade. This demand far exceeds supply, and has precipitated a global education crisis that, if not corrected, will put 4.5 trillion US dollars of the global GDP at risk by 2016 (Project Management Institute, 2011).

Impact of Project Management on Effective Business Performance

The role of project management is to help a firm advance and be ahead of its competition, develop complex products or services in a very short time and capture new markets. In such a business scenario, project management becomes a powerful tool in the hands of the organization that is aware of the conditions in its environment, and its implementation requires specific competencies. Thus the development of project management in the organization together with the implementation of information technology management permits the organization's team to define plans, manage projects and synchronize team tasks, resource allocation, and so on. In addition, there must be a predetermined standard against which individual and group performances are measured in order to determine operational efficiency or productivity at an appropriate time.

The importance of project-based modes organizing work has been recognized in a wide range of industries and project-based modes have even been said to represent a new logic of organizing in market-based economics. Aerospace and defence, for example, are extremely project-intensive, working for years on long-term contracts or development projects that will eventually bring forth a new jet aircraft, missile system, ship or piece of electronic wizardry. Likewise, almost by definition, construction is another industry that exhibits a high degree of project activity. Food, retailing and textiles, on the other hand, are less project-intensive (Wheatley, 2009).

Implementation of project management in the organization is rather broad and includes all types of projects, from the simplest ones to the most complex. Hence there are an increasing number of companies that implement the project as their basic management strategy. Thus projects become a new strategic option for the organizational design of the company, whose ultimate goal is to achieve "project excellence". This in turn means the organizational environment is permeated by a continual tendency to manage projects successfully. In order that this is achieved and the project-oriented organization is created, it is necessary that project management and project portfolio management be implemented.

In order to achieve the highest level of effectiveness from project management, it is critical that the approach is applied to the entire structure of the organization, not just to a certain division, department or staff level.

Applying effective project management for deployment of strategy and goals can thus provide organizations the following advantages:

- business advantage through timely achievement of goals and optimal resource utilization based on decision making;

- competitive advantage through a workforce energized by a culture of execution and collaboration, and customers satisfied by getting the "right" results regularly.

Measuring the project's success can be conducted on the basis of the following parameters (Radović-Marković, 2012):

- on the basis of the end results of the project (products or services), including the quality and the extent to which all requirements are met;

- on the basis of the method through which the project is organized, structured and managed, including the cost control, the efficiency of the project plan, and so on;

- on the basis of the human resources that are an important constituent of every project, including the resource utilization and the relationships among the team members.

These three parameters on the basis of which the project success is measured may vary, depending on the type of the project. For these reasons, the criteria of success should be stated for each project separately and be adjusted to specific project conditions.

All the criteria for success must be stated in a simple way, and once they have been defined, priorities must be set. At the end of the project, the success criterion can be used in evaluating the project performances. If this is viewed from only one perspective, important indicators for improving the future performances may be missing.

In addition, project management is of little value if it is not incorporated into the overall strategy of the business.

Conclusions

Success of project-based firms depends primarily on the competency of project management, much more than on technological competencies. It means that the project management can make the greatest contribution to the success of the organization, if it the mission, vision and priorities are clear.

The following steps are necessary for project management to make a greater impact on the improvement of business performance:

- implement the project management methodology adjusted to organizational needs and culture;

- train and educate the employees at all key positions in the organization to implement project management;

- manage key functions;

- train to manage a set of projects;

- create a transparent link between the company strategy and the key projects;

- create an appropriate organizational design, IT structure and management processes.

The specialized role of project management is in bringing support to organizations that want to innovate, whether for new products or for new business initiatives. Thus, it is necessary to foster more research on innovation in project-based organizations.

References

Kujala, J., Gemünden, H.G. and Lechler, T. (2012). *Organizing in projects and temporary organizations*. Retrieved January 2012 from http://www.egos2012.net/2011/06/sub-theme-53-organizing-in-projects-and-temporary-organizations/.

Project Management Institute (2011). Retrieved February 2012 from http://www.pmiteach.org/.

Radović-Marković, M. (2007). *Global Management*. Belgrade, Serbia: Magnus.

Radović-Marković, M. (2012). *Impact of Globalization on Organizational Culture, Behavior and Gender Role*. Charlotte, NC: IAP.

Radović-Marković, M. and Omolaja, M. (2011). *Management Dynamics in the New Economy*. Saarbrücken, Germany: VDM Verlag Dr. Müller.

Shenhar, A.J. and Dvir, D. (2007). Project management research – The challenge and opportunity. *International Journal of Project Management, 38*(2), 93–99.

Wheatley, M. (2009). *The importance of project management*. Retrieved January 2010 from http://www.projectsmart.co.uk/the-importance-of-project-management.html.

Whitley, R. (2006). Project-based firms: new organizational form or variations on a theme. *Industrial and Corporate Change, 15*(1), 77–99.

Home-based Firms

Introduction

Thinking "entrepreneurially" leads to the intention to start a business and ultimately to the decision to act on that intention (Busenitz and Lau, 1996). Entrepreneurship is an integrated concept that permeates an individual's business in an innovative manner. Different theoretical approaches to entrepreneurship show that this field of research is very broad. Understanding entrepreneurial learning and education is critical (Cope, 2005; Gartner and Birney, 2002; Mitchell et al., 2002) to support the acquisition of knowledge and skills required for sustainable business development. However, research that examines the "complex interactive learning relationship that exists between the entrepreneur, her/his business and the wider environment" (Cope, 2005) is still in the early stages of development (Minniti and Bygrave, 2001; Ravasi and Turati, 2005).

Considering the importance of education for entrepreneurs, it has recently become evident that the current generation is looking for new forms of education, such as creative education. Creative education and training should help entrepreneurs to raise their creativity, logical thinking and entrepreneurship skills/capabilities/performance (Radović-Marković, 2012). Many scientists think that knowledge is the most important requirement for business success and so it is the factor receiving the most attention.

Recent research in the United States shows that business owners who were not educated enough for the business in which they are engaged were not successful, that is, more than 80 per cent of their businesses failed during the first year of its existence (Radović-Marković, 2009). On the contrary, those entrepreneurs who were sufficiently educated and who showed constant interest in improvement have increased their business success (60 per cent) after the completion of basic training programmes for entrepreneurship.

Certain skills cannot be developed solely through simple multiple-choice exams. New education programmes for entrepreneurs must be based on exchanging good practices through studies and networks among strategic partners (researchers, entrepreneurs, financiers, advisors, policy-makers and so forth).

Becoming an entrepreneur, however, is a time-consuming process, and the goal of education is not only to rush students into becoming entrepreneurs, but rather to provide them with tools that enable realistic student self-evaluations, even several years after graduation.

Home Business Opportunities

Starting an entrepreneurial venture is an avenue that more and more women and men are pursuing for a variety of reasons. One of those reasons is the ability to create a schedule that accommodates work and family. In addition, increasing job demands, the blurring of boundaries between work and home life, declining job security and flat earnings have made this more challenging for men (Aumann et al., 2011). Furthermore, many families need to start a business as a source of additional income. Work options that can provide home business opportunities include part time, flex time, telecommuting, compressed workweek (full time in three or four days), freelance and consulting, job-sharing with other family members and so forth.

The "typical" family today is very different. Many parents today pursue careers and raise families at the same time. This is a very different picture than half a century ago. There are five million stay-at-home mums compared to 176,000 stay-at-home dads; that is they only account for 3.4 per cent of stay-at-home parents (Chiaramonte, 2012). Despite a significantly higher proportion of women working from home than men, the number of stay-at-home dads in the United States has tripled in the last decade. According to the results of a new study by Boston College (Harrington et al., 2012), the rise of stay-at-home dads may be more a result of choices and evolving gender roles of parents. This study shows that the large proportion of fathers who would consider this option indicates potential for further growth in the at-home dad population in the future (Harrington et al., 2012).

Most home-based entrepreneurs are engaged in the professional and services industry. In addition, there are dozens of popular hobbies that can be turned into home business – writing, photography, catering, raising animals, gardening, genealogy and crafts of all kinds are just a few examples. Namely, a hobby can serve as a source of a new idea, that is, a hobby often grows into a new business, which becomes the entrepreneur's basic business decision. We will give an example of how a hobby in genealogy can turn into lucrative and viable home-based business.

Turning a Hobby into a Home-based Business – The Case of Genealogy

A Bank of America analysis reported "Nine million internet users describe genealogy as a 'core passion/hobby,' and the majority of these (7.5 million) are 45 years and older." According to Archive.com (2012), which offers "family history made simple and affordable", about 65 per cent of its members are female and only 35 per cent are male. A Harris Interactive (2009) survey estimated that 87 per cent of American adults are interested in learning about their family histories. Despite genealogy being considered a hobby, there are many entrepreneurial opportunities for genealogists. Advantages of this business include that one can start it with a minimum investment (2,000–10,000 US dollars), do it part time and from home.

Businesses that genealogists and other entrepreneurs do in their homes are relatively new. According to many indicators, these businesses are very stable, which is affirmed by data that show that the average age of businesses that owners run from their homes is around six years (Radović-Marković, 2009). The research also showed that workers who work at home use computers and modern technologies to do their everyday tasks more than in other types of businesses. In this way, by opening the door to modern technology and by using it in every day work situations, they have gained more opportunities in choosing businesses that best suit their life style and have made running a business much easier (Radović-Marković and Kyaruzi, 2010).

Internet services, in conjunction with more widely-used communication media, provide the broadest enhancement of information and communication resources. Namely, today genealogists have access to capabilities that make it remarkably easy for many people with a casual interest in genealogy to quickly assemble an accurate view of their family history (Voelker, 2011).

Many genealogists are still working towards converting their hobby into their career. The genealogist business is varied and an entrepreneur can choose the genealogy business according to his/her specialty – in order to design and run genealogical websites, research family history or to conduct family history consultations.

Rules for Running a Home Business

It is not easy to work from home, although it may seem so at the first sight. Many people have a vision that a business at home should provide plenty of time for relaxing, socializing, dealing with family members/affairs and other personal activities. They expect that this will enable them to avoid long business meetings, criticisms of bosses and so on.

However, although work from home allows more freedom and different opportunities for quality use of time, business owners still fall into traps, because they lack organizational capabilities and cannot organize their commitments and time. In order to succeed in realizing one's business intentions and to avoid the traps of running business at home, we list several rules below to follow:

- First, energize your entrepreneurial idea by initiating it and turning it into solid activities. Next, think of how your business will be unique and think of an original way to maximize the service for customers. In other words, the customers must always have your full attention. It is well known that every business is born with a product or a service and that it dies without customers. Therefore, no matter what type of business is initiated, whether it is an e-business or a traditional one, it is important to maintain control of all its operations and resources. Among those, customers are considered the greatest of all resources. It is thus vital to connect to your customers and offer them a reason to come back to you. It is then very important to create a positive experience for them, out of everything the customers sees and in which they takes part. Always have in mind that your customers' positive experience is the key to the success of any small business.

- Emphasize the uniqueness of your service. Find a market that does not have high-quality services and offer something new and original. You must also become a technical fanatic; take advantage of the latest technological achievements, which should help your business to improve and develop. Continually innovate and redesign your web presentation and work on it in order to make it more interesting for a larger number of visitors, while also connecting with them. Connection to the external world through the Internet is vitally important, as well as connection through professional associations, organizations and such.

- Structure your time. It is vital to organize your time well in order not to overlap private and business activities, and always form business priorities. Try to minimize the time you spend outside your office during working hours.

- Use services of experts and practice team work. Form a team of experts and external associates that can support you when necessary for your genealogy research. Monthly meetings with associates are recommended, at which all business opportunities, challenges and potential mistakes can be discussed.

- Do not avoid changes. They are often desirable in some elements of your work. Also, the opinions of associates should be taken into account, because they bring mistakes to your attention as well as offer, suggestions and opinions. Whenever possible, then, corrections and changes should be accepted.

We can distinguish between two types of changes: reactive changes, which are necessary when responding to research problems (technical errors, the lack of resources, and so on), and requested changes, which may arise from new ideas, new information or new business perspectives. The role of the knowledge of entrepreneurs is the most significant; keeping in mind that management of changes is a very risky and sensitive process that demands a combination of planning and communication skills, logical and creative capabilities, working experience, and so on. These skills are necessary, regardless of the type of project and the level of changes being implemented.

The genealogist's responsibilities are as follows:

- identify projects, research requirements and determine an appropriate procedure for gathering project documentation;

- determine the type of project documentation required, considering project plans, contracts, technical documentation, work specification, reports, and so on;

- determine how and when gathered documentation will be used;

- determine who will enter the data on the prepared forms;

- determine how documentation will be used, given its complexity and the size of the project;

- determine the software to be used;

- define the importance of documents;

- determine how to analyse the documents.

However, the tasks that all genealogists have in common are to define the documentation required, gather and analyse it and make it available to customers on time. Managing these activities can be interpreted as having the ability, mind set and the skills that are essential for success. This requires much knowledge, technical skills and experience, and above all, their proper integration into a whole, which should lead to the use of human and financial resources necessary to achieve business results.

Key Decisions to Initiate a Home Business

A good business plan should be developed with the intention to explore all the possibilities defined for a business. This may be the most difficult phase of the entrepreneurial process. The parts of a typical business plan are: mission, overview of key objectives, the market environment, strategy, financial forecast and activity. A business plan is conducted at the beginning of each business year and must be done professionally, which requires hiring managers and entrepreneurs, as well as a number of consultants or specialized agencies. A business plan, according to some estimates, requires more than 200 hours to prepare. It has to give a potential investor a complete picture and understanding of the new business and clarify important components of the business.

The size of a business plan mostly depends on the amount of the investment required in the planned business. The more resources that are required, the more details must be included in the business plan and the more estimates and suggestions should be included. The realistic average size of a business plan is three to ten pages, which accents the most important business details with related financial estimates. Creating a formal business plan consumes both time and resources.

After the business plan is prepared, it should be checked again to evaluate whether the choice of the business suits the market and the interests and desires of the future business owner(s). That is, to what extent do personal and market interests overlap? At this stage, the most important thing is to balance the entrepreneur's personal goals with market demands.

Many entrepreneurs start their home business part time, as a result of raising their children and other family commitments. Others cannot be engaged more than a few hours per day, since their home business is an additional or second job, that is, they have other work obligations. Entrepreneurs usually decide to work from home on a full-time basis when family and financial conditions permit them to do so. Thus, they have maximum dedication to their home business, giving their full attention to it, as well as their time, knowledge and money.

However, there are many entrepreneurs who do not pay attention to this decision, since they do not consider it important. Instead, they expect to decide in time, after the business is functioning and, depending on the scope of activities, how much time they would dedicate daily to the home-business activities. Thus, they can choose between working full time or part time. When making such a decision, one should realistically consider their family situation, finances and the amount of spare time that the entrepreneur can dedicate to the new enterprise (Radović –Marković, 2009).

Sometimes it is very hard to make a clear distinction between part-time and full-time employment, keeping in mind that most home-business owners spend the majority of their spare and work time thinking about their business – about marketing strategies, planning and similar issues. Therefore, it is common that the entrepreneur seamlessly goes over that boundary, and begins to dedicate himself/herself to it full time.

Most genealogists work part time. According to the US Bureau of Labor Statistics, 57 per cent of genealogists worked part time, while only 34 per cent worked full time in 1997 (Rada, 2011). In other words, many genealogists are self-employed and work on a contractual basis for their clients. Even though, part-time engagement gives more work freedom and provides many personal options. The practice in numerous countries has shown (including the US and other countries with a long tradition of doing business from home) that engagement of this kind is short-lived, and it rapidly grows to full-time employment.

Full-time employment shows certain advantages: higher degree of professionalism in business; faster business development and increase in market share. Despite the advantages, some disadvantages could also be mentioned for full-time engagement. Among the main disadvantages are: greater risk, higher initial costs and loss of additional job (Radović-Marković and Kyaruzi, 2010).

These disadvantages did not significantly contribute to home-business owners becoming discouraged and giving up full-time dedication to their work. Many of them hold on to the well-known business proverb, "no great risk in business – no great gain". A genealogist's annual earnings may vary considerably depending upon her/his client base and, the size of projects to which she/he is assigned. Of all professional genealogists, 50 per cent have average salaries between $22,880 and $52,041 as of January 2011, according to PayScale (Schnotz, 2011).

Determination of Success or Failure of a Home Business

It is logical to expect that everyone who starts a new business wishes that it succeeds, regardless of the type of business and the way it is organized and run. But, what does it mean to be successful in business? As an entrepreneur, this is a question that you are expected to ask yourself, keeping in mind that you spend your energy, time and money, as well as talent, to create a new business. Actually, despite all your efforts, experience and knowledge, it may seem sometimes that your business is not going the way you want and as you expected.

Self-evaluations are thus important, and should be a part of your daily management process. Learning "how you work" may be an excellent basis for deciding which route to take next. There are several tests that can help determine how good or bad your business is. One must keep in mind that the success of a five-year-old business cannot be evaluated in the same way as the one that is only six months old, which is practically in the phase of development/incubation.

Some of these ways to determine the route the business is on are:

- Have you achieved all your planned goals? Compare your business plan with your results. Also compare performances of your business to competition businesses. Determine your part of the market.

- Do you pay your bills regularly? One of the main indicators of your business's success is whether you are in a position to cover your expenses on time. If you are, you may consider your business as functioning well. If you are not able to fulfil these commitments, then it is necessary to take certain steps and make efforts to improve your business activities. Maybe the only thing you have to do is decrease your expenses, or maybe your choice of business was wrong. Also, do not expect that you can make so much money in the phase of development that you can fulfil the desires, for which you founded the business. The advice for all those who enter entrepreneurial waters is to be patient and to do your work well. If you do, your business will certainly fulfil your material and other expectations in the long term.

- Have you accomplished more as an entrepreneur or when you were employed by someone else? Many entrepreneurs start their own business because they are not satisfied with their job and/or with their, material and social status. Therefore, when you enter entrepreneurial waters, you must ask yourself whether you earn more now than when you were working for someone else. You should also compare earnings of your colleagues who run similar businesses, have similar education and working experience as an entrepreneur. All these answers will provide an excellent index of whether you are more successful now than when you were employed by someone else. The evaluation of your success, as well as deciding whether the existing business should be modified in some segments or replaced with another, will depend on those answers.

- What does a financial report show? A simple financial ratio analysis is the best way to show the financial weaknesses and advantages of your business.

- How are the sales doing? The trend of the sales of your products must be examined by comparing the data with the previous month and the previous year. If you notice a constant decrease of your sales, you must make a different sales strategy. Actually, these data should show whether your marketing efforts are efficient, whether the distribution mechanisms are operating well and whether there is still demand for your products or services.

- Do you make a profit? Do you lose or earn money? When can you expect profit from your business? Do you have sufficient financial means to cover expenses while your business is without profit? In the long term, is your business profitable at all?

- How do you feel about your business? Maybe the answer to this question is one of the best indexes of whether your business is successful or not. Actually, many entrepreneurs start their business for different motives. Some of them have already been mentioned, but the one of extreme importance is whether the business is approached with the same passion as it was at the beginning?

At the end of this analysis you may conclude whether or not your business is worth your engagement and effort. But, only the business that fulfils you in every way and makes you happy can bring you success.

Conclusions

The new economy is often seen as something just dependent upon the Internet. In truth, it does rely on good information, but also hugely on the exercise of entrepreneurial skills. Even small business owners now face the continuous task of acquiring knowledge and monitoring the worldwide competition. They must find the right formula to find a market, meet customers' demands and offer services at the best prices possible. Networking, information gathering and learning – in other words "researching" – form a huge part of any successful entrepreneurial endeavour.

Genealogy serves as a good example of something lending itself to running a small home-based business. Having agreed that the success of small home-based firms depends primarily on the "research" competency of their entrepreneur owners, it is only natural that the research skills that are critical in the field of genealogy will stand the entrepreneurial home-based business owner in good stead. So, genealogists stand a good chance of making their research a genuine voyage of discovery as well as their business innovation.

This is but one example of where something that starts out as a hobby might enable an entrepreneur to turn their dreams into a successful and profitable business.

References

Archive.com (2012). *Online family history trends*, 2 February [Web log message]. Retrieved 3 March 2012 from http://www.archives.com/blog/miscellaneous/ online-family-history-trends-1.html#_ednref9.

Aumann, K., Galinsky, E. and Matos, K. (2011). *The New Male Mystique*. New York: Families and Work Institute.

Busenitz, L.W. and Lau, C.M. (1996). A cross-cultural cognitive model of new venture creation. *Entrepreneurship Theory and Practice, 20*(4), 25–39.

Chiaramonte, P. (2012). *Mr. Mom Era: Stay-at-home dads doubled over last decade. Foxnews.* Retrieved 2 November 2012 from http://www.foxnews. com/us/2012/06/17/mr-mom-era-stay-at-home-dads-doubled-over-last- decade/#ixzz2FhXI0uog.

Compete.com, Findagrave.com, Familysearch.org, Rootsweb.com, USGW Archives.net, Cyndislist.com, USgenweb.org. Retrieved February 2012 from http://www.compete.com/.

Cope, J. (2005). Toward a dynamic learning perspective of entrepreneurship. *Entrepreneurship Theory and Practice, 29*(4), 373–397.

Gartner, W.B. and Birney, S. (2002). Introduction to the special issue on qualitative methods in entrepreneurship research. *Journal of Business Venturing, 17*, 387–395.

Harrington, B., Van Deusen, F. and Mazar, I. (2012). *The New Dad: Right at Home.* Boston, MA: Boston College.

Harris Interactive (2009). *Harris Interactive Survey*, July. Retrieved October 2010 from http://corporate.ancestry.com/library/media/Getting%20Started%20 One-Sheet%202.19.10.pdf.

Minniti, M. and Bygrave, W. (2001). A dynamic model of entrepreneurial learning. *Entrepreneurship: Theory and Practice, 23*(4), 41–52.

Mitchell, R., Busenitz, L., Lant, T., McDougall, P.P., Morse, E.A. and Smith, J.B. (2002). Toward a theory of entrepreneurial cognition: Rethinking the people side of entrepreneurship research. *Entrepreneurship Theory and Practice, 27*(2), 93–104.

Rada. J. (2011). *How much does a genealogist make?* Retrieved 28 December 2011 from http://www.ehow.com/info_7942342_much-genealogist-make.html#ixzz1ljOzOLG4.

Radović-Marković, M. (2009). *Women Entrepreneurs: New Opportunities and Challenges.* Delhi, India: Indo-American Books.

Radović-Marković, M. (2012). *Impact of Globalization on Organizational Culture, Behaviour and Gender Role.* Charlotte, NC: IAP.

Radović-Marković, M. and Kyaruzi, I.S. (2010). *Women in Business: Theory, Practice and Flexible Approaches.* London: Adonis and Abbey.

Ravasi, D. and Turati, C. (2005). Exploring entrepreneurial learning: A comparative study of technology development projects. *Journal of Business Venturing, 20*(1), 137–164.

Schnotz, W. (2011). *Professional genealogist salary.* Retrieved January 2012 from http://www.ehow.com/info_7805586_professional-genealogist-salary.html.

Voelker, D. (2011). *Serial entrepreneurship and genealogy, genealogy industry,* Retrieved March 2012 from http://www.digicopia.com/serial-entrepreneurship-genealogy/.

Index

Methodology of the Study

Project-based Firms

If you have found this book useful you may be interested in other titles from Gower

Father-Daughter Succession in Family Business:
A Cross-Cultural Perspective
Edited by Daphne Halkias, Paul W. Thurman, Celina Smith
and Robert S. Nason
Hardback: 978-0-566-09220-6
Ebook – PDF: 978-0-566-09221-3
Ebook – ePUB: 978-1-4094-5973-6

Entrepreneurship, Innovation and Business Clusters
Panos G. Piperopoulos
Hardback: 978-1-4094-3442-9
Ebook – PDF: 978-1-4094-3443-6
Ebook – ePUB: 978-1-4094-8697-8

Government, SMEs and Entrepreneurship Development:
Policy, Practice and Challenges
Edited by Robert A. Blackburn and Michael T. Schaper
Hardback: 978-1-4094-3035-3
Ebook– PDF: 978-1-4094-3036-0
Ebook – ePUB: 978-1-4094-8408-0

Creating and Re-Creating Corporate
Entrepreneurial Culture
Alzira Salama
Hardback: 978-0-566-09194-0
Ebook – PDF: 978-0-566-09195-7
Ebook – ePUB: 978-1-4094-5968-2

GOWER